THE ART OF PLAIN TALK

The Art of
PLAIN TALK

BY RUDOLF FLESCH, PH.D.
Author of "Marks of Readable Style"

FOREWORD BY
LYMAN BRYSON
Educational Director
Columbia Broadcasting System

HARPER & BROTHERS PUBLISHERS
New York and London

THE ART OF PLAIN TALK

Printed in the United States of America

F-W

To Elizabeth

Contents

Contents

Foreword

By Lyman Bryson
Educational Director
Columbia Broadcasting System

Anyone who undertakes to write a word of introduction to Rudolf Flesch's book should make sure before he begins that he has something to say and can put it in plain words. I have seen Dr. Flesch grow in mastery of the tricky problems of readability and I feel an avuncular (beg pardon) an uncle-like pride in his achievements. On that account, I am willing to risk putting a few words of my own ahead of his although his book, in every way, speaks for itself.

It might be worth a moment of a reader's time to be told that the deceptive ease and clarity in Dr. Flesch's writing are not only the showing of his own skill; they are also the result of his acquaintance with scientific studies in the psychology of verbal communication. Gray, Thorndike, Lorge, Dale, Strang, Gates and Flesch himself, among all the others, have made advances in finding out what readers get, and what they do not get, out of looking at black marks on a white page.

It is not only that investigators have discovered that many young people go through school, or are pushed through, without ever really learning to read. That is true, of course, and our so-called literacy is only a shallow statistical fact. Many people can read, haltingly, if they must, but they do not have enough skill to enjoy it. They would rather look at pictures. Whether or not they understand the pictures is another question. And yet these people, millions of them, vote and run machinery and handle the dangerous gadgets of a civilization of which they understand very little. Only those who have made or followed special investigations know the extent of this real illiteracy.

They ought to be taught to read. They are not lacking in

intelligence and they ought to be taught to read. But when we have granted that, what do we do about it? Send them back to school? By whose orders? They certainly will not go on their own initiative. Do better with the next generation? Of course, that is a possible achievement. In the meantime, there is one thing we can do, and that is to see that a few books on important subjects get written in language that they —these millions of amiable but letter-blind friends—can follow. More than that, we can see that the books they need to read, the documents they have to understand, the instructions that will keep them out of trouble, are written in plain English.

There is nothing anti-literary in such a suggestion. In the great stream of English literature there are two lines, one ornate, the other plain, and surely no one will say that Swift was less than Sir Thomas Browne. And, in any case, the improvement of writing in official documents and signs would be toward plainness and clarity if it could be achieved at all. Remember the now fading signs of the war years, "Illumination is required to be extinguished before these premises are closed to business." Are those the sacred accents of literature?

As a matter of fact, all the argument against readable books on the ground of literary taste would still be beside the point if it had any value. The help that Dr. Flesch is offering to struggling writers is not for those whose business it is to create literature. We live, unluckily perhaps, in a world where a good deal of public and private business has to be done in print or in typescript. Nearly everybody must "write." And in most of these routine matters the one virtue that is important, and seldom shown, is to be understood.

The scientists began some years ago to discover the real nature of unreadability. Dr. Flesch is here trying something that goes beyond diagnostic studies and is probably more difficult. He is offering sound and practical "rules" for producing the readable kind of writing, stepping out of the role of scientist and becoming a teacher and giving a good example of the skill he is trying to teach. There are a good many teachers in our secondary schools who would get further in their task of making literate young men and women out of careless boys and girls if they could understand and inculcate the principles set forth in this brief book. And in the field of public affairs it might be said, with bated breath, that some composers of government orders, some orators in the cause of labor, some public relations men on business payrolls, could profit by the use of these rules. We might go so far as to say that diplomats and politicians, too, could get some good out of these exercises in plain speaking if we could be sure that they desire to be clearly understood.

Writing for any practical purpose is a difficult and elusive art. Anyone who can, as Rudolf Flesch has done, make our success more likely, deserves our gratitude and our respectful attention.

Preface

About two years ago, I published my Ph.D. dissertation "Marks of Readable Style," which contained a statistical formula for measuring readability. The dissertation was quite a success, as dissertations go, and the formula is now being used in many organizations and government agencies. This has been gratifying, but also somewhat embarrassing to me: for "Marks of Readable Style," being a Ph.D. dissertation, was not a very readable book. I tried to rewrite it in simple language, but when I was through, a natural thing had happened and I had written a new book. This is the book.

Its main feature is, of course, the formula. I almost wish it were not. Some readers, I am afraid, will expect a magic formula for good writing and will be disappointed with my simple yardstick. Others, with a passion for accuracy, will wallow in the little rules and computations but lose sight of the principles of plain English. What I hope for are readers who won't take the formula too seriously and won't expect from it more than a rough estimate.

The other features of the book are not particularly novel, but may seem novel to people who have been trained in conventional rhetoric and composition. Some of these will doubtless accuse me of advocating "bad grammar." I have found that the simplest answer to such purists is to ask how often they use the "correct" form "Should you like to wash your hands?" The realization that everyone in America says "Would you like . . ." is a good starting point for a discussion of the difference between conventional grammar and linguistic facts.

During the last few years, I have been dealing with simple language as a researcher, librarian, teacher, editor, and writer. Naturally, I had all five of these professions in mind when I wrote the book. I hope it will be useful to each.

R. F.

Acknowledgments

I wish to thank the following persons and organizations for their kind permission to use copyrighted material:

Mr. Lyman Bryson and the Columbia Broadcasting System for the excerpt from *The People's Platform* (August 21, 1943); The Viking Press for two quotations from *Reflections on the Revolution of Our Time* by Harold J. Laski; Mr. George Bernard Shaw for the quotation from his *Intelligent Woman's Guide to Socialism and Capitalism*; *Time* for quotations from that magazine; *The Saturday Review of Literature* for quotations from that magazine; *The Washington Post* for quotations from "Mary Haworth's Mail" and from the editorial "Boning Up" (December 9, 1944); Scripps-Howard Newspapers for the quotation from Ernie Pyle's column "It's the Infantry" (August 12, 1944); *The New York Times* for the excerpt from the editorial "This Land and Flag" (June 14, 1940); Mr. Samuel Grafton for the excerpt from his column "I'd Rather Be Right" (December 8, 1943); *The New Yorker* for quotations from that magazine; Mr. Paul de Kruif and Harcourt, Brace & Company for the quotations from the book *Microbe Hunters*; Mr. Walter B. Pitkin and *The Reader's Digest* for the quotation from the article "In a Great Man's Shoes" (*Reader's Digest,* October 1940); Mr. Leo M. Cherne for the quotation from his book "The Rest of Your Life"; Mr. Maury Maverick and *The New York Times* for the article "The Case Against Gobbledygook" (*New York Times Magazine,* May 21, 1944); Mr. J. D. Ratcliff and *The Reader's Digest* for the excerpts from the article "The Yellow Magic of Penicillin" (*Reader's Digest,* August 1943); the American Book Company for excerpts from *The Development of America* by Fremont P. Wirth; Dr. Thomas H. Briggs for the quotations from his article "How to Write Books for High-School Pupils" (*School & Society,* May 8, 1943); Brandt & Brandt for the quotation from *America* by Stephen Vincent Benét; D. C. Heath & Company for the quotation from *Robert Louis Stevenson's Treasure Island,* adapted by T. E. Dunshee and Minna Ludeke; and the J. B. Lippincott Company for the quotation from *Young Man-of-the-House* by Mabel Leigh Hunt.

R. F.

Chapter I

PLAIN TALK IS AN ART

THIS is a book on plain talk. It tells you how to speak and write so that people understand what you mean.

If you never write anything and never talk to anybody but your family or maybe a few friends and neighbors, you won't need this book. Your listeners will tell you if they don't understand; or they will frown, or look puzzled, or just blank. You will never be in doubt whether what you say is plain: if it isn't, you will have to repeat it until it is.

But people who never talk to more than half a dozen others at a time are rare. The chances are you are not one of them; rather, you are someone who has to make speeches, address meetings, give lectures and radio talks, write letters or reports or articles or books. All these things mean that you have to talk to an audience who can't talk back. You cannot even look at them to see whether they understand or not. For all you know, they may screw up their faces, or shrug their shoulders, or turn away, unable to make head or tail of anything you say. But you can't see them because they are way down at the far end of the hall; or thousands of miles away sitting before a radio; or separated from you by weeks or months when they read what you wrote. There is nothing more important to you as a speaker and writer than that your audience understand you; and on just this point you can never be sure. You are forever guessing.

This is unfortunate. It means that you may never learn how to make yourself better understood. As long as you are just guessing, you have no way of knowing whether your guess was good or bad, and whether you are getting better or worse.

What you need is a check on your performance; without a check, you can't learn anything. This is an important psychological principle; it was proved a few years ago in an interesting experiment by Professor E. L. Thorndike. What he did was this: he took a student and told him to draw, blindfold, lines exactly four inches long. For days and days, the student tried; but there was no sign of progress. The length of his lines remained a matter of pure chance. The reason was, of course, that Professor Thorndike never told him how long his lines were. He had no yardstick; therefore he could not learn.

As a speaker and writer, you are well equipped with yardsticks and standards and rules for things like grammar or spelling or usage; you can make sure, beyond doubt, that *lay* is the past tense of *to lie,* or that *analyzed* is spelled with a *y,* or that *all right* is written as two words. All these things you can learn simply by looking them up in a reference book and making it a habit to follow the rule. But if you want to make sure that your listeners or readers will understand, these books won't help you. If your readers feel that you are too highbrow for them, they won't be satisfied if you tell them that you used Roget's *Thesaurus* or Webster's *Dictionary.* What you need is a reference book on simple language; and you won't find such a book on your desk.

To be sure, it is not hard to find advice on how to write. There are thousands of books on that subject. After all, books are written by people whose business is writing and who are as eager to talk shop as anybody else. You can go for your advice to Aristotle's *Rhetoric* or to Schopenhauer's *Essay on Style,* to modern authors like W. Somerset Maugham (*The Summing Up*) or Stephen Leacock (*How to Write*), or to countless others who set down their experience in working with words.

They all agree on how to make people understand. They all tell you to be simple, to use ordinary, plain language, to make your sentences short, and to use familiar, everyday words. After you have read a dozen or so books on style and writing, you get tired of such general suggestions and impatient to know just how you go about being simple, how you can make sentences short, and how you can tell a familiar word.

At that point you will probably turn to textbooks on composition, handbooks on usage, and so on. But you are in for a disappointment. Their suggestions are usually just as vague as those by the great writers, and, if specific, they are likely to be arbitrary and often ridiculous.

Here, for instance, is a recent 820-page college textbook on English composition, written by four university professors. You look up "Style" and find this:

> A familiar style is created through the use of familiar words, which are usually short, Saxon words. . . . It is frequently desirable to use the longer word because it is more precise or more cultured than the short word; but vigor and ease are often sacrificed when the rugged Saxon word is supplanted by the Latinistic word. . . .

So their tip is to use words with Saxon rather than Latin roots. But how can you take such advice seriously, when it comes out of an ivory tower where Saxon words are spoken of as "rugged"? If you follow the four professors, then *indeed, writer,* and *undertaker* are "rugged," and *in fact, author* and *mortician* are "more precise and more cultured." But Saxon words *are* usually short and easy, you say. Of course they are; and so are *face, pear,* and *street,* which come from Latin.

But maybe you are prejudiced against textbooks anyhow; maybe you would go for advice to one of those handbooks on speaking and writing that are written for adults. Let us look at a recent book on English usage by a famous literary critic. Under the heading "Compactness" we find the following rule:

> Make your sentences compact. Use a word to do the work of a phrase when possible without loss to the idea intended. The sentence *She ran down the corridor in haste* may without the slightest loss of meaning be more economically stated thus: *She ran down the corridor hastily.*

That's economy for you: two syllables made into three, and the colloquial *in haste* replaced by the literary *hastily*. If you follow this rule you can be sure of only one thing: you'll make it harder for your reader.

Occasionally, however, you come upon hints on simple language that seem to be straight out of the horse's mouth. You see no reason why you shouldn't trust an article on "Two-Syllable Science," written by a man who prepares instruction booklets for a leading automobile manufacturer. This man, if anybody, must know the secrets of simple language, you think. Here is what he says:

> There are numerous devices that help create the type of atmosphere desired in this kind of booklet. One, for example, is the use of the word *incidentally* in introducing a further step in the development of the story. Footnotes offer a convenient means of conveying information in a casual manner.

This would be just funny if it were not for the fact that the writer may still be at large explaining the workings of your car with clever *incidentallys* and "casual" footnotes. And what's more, there are probably many other writers who read his article and use his ideas now for their own copy.

Anyway, here you are trying to find advice on simple language, and all you get is generalities, or the suggestion of putting "rugged," "compact" words "casually" in a footnote.

You will find no such nonsense in this book. To be sure, I shall give you specific suggestions on how to build your sentences and how to choose your words; but these rules will never be arbitrary. In other words, this book contains only advice that is based on scientific evidence; if you follow it, you can be certain that people will understand you better.

Why? Well, try to think of simple language in terms of industrial research. When a plastics manufacturer, say, gets interested in producing a new kind of material that will stand a certain amount of stress, pressure, and heat, the chemists in their laboratories go to work to find the right formula. They start with the idea that a certain combination of elements might do the trick, put it together, and test it for stress, pressure, and heat. If the new plastic stands all the tests, it is put in production, and in due course it appears on the market.

There is no reason why you can't apply the same principle to language. Suppose you want to write something for boys in fifth grade. You have a notion that understanding has something to do with the length of the sentences, and so you take a number of stories with sentences of various length and let a group of fifth-grade boys read them. Next you ask the boys questions to test whether they understood each story; and then you find the average sentence length of those stories all of them understood. Result: if you write for boys in fifth grade, your average sentence should contain so-and-so many words.

Now, if you apply this technique to a large number of language elements, and to many different types of readers and listeners, you can work out exact style formulas for whatever audience you have to talk to. This book is really a collection of such formulas or recipes in convenient form.

One more general scientific principle has been used for this book. Science, as you know, is international. It cuts across national borderlines in a real sense: experiments carried out in Sweden are followed up in England and tested in America. If a scientific fact has been verified once, it may be used anywhere. You may wonder how this principle can be applied to language research, since each nation speaks differently. But the fundamentals of language and the psychology of human speech are the same everywhere; and if one country adopts a practical, simple linguistic device, it might well be transferred to another language. Take, for instance, Modern Persian which has done away with articles: exactly the same simplification is being used today by our headline writers who write RED ARMY TAKES KIEV instead of THE RED ARMY TAKES KIEV. Of course, they are not consciously imitating Persian; but in other instances, this might not be a bad idea. So, in this book, you will find quite a few recommendations that are based on practices in foreign languages.

But maybe you don't care for scientific rules in your speaking and writing. Maybe you have been teaching for twenty years and trust your experience, or you are a young writer and feel sure of your natural gift for simple language. If you have that gift, you may be justly proud. It is rare, and people like Paul De Kruif and Stuart Chase are paid well for their unusual skill. Less gifted popularizers, as a rule, rely on some makeshift device to keep in touch with their audience. One well-known writer of juveniles writes all her books for her eight-year-old nephew Tommy; another experienced platform speaker makes it a habit to address an old man somewhere in the tenth or twelfth row to the left. Such schemes may work well; but in the end their success depends upon your own power of imagination.

In fact, nothing but a scientific check can keep you from forgetting your audience while you are speaking or writing. It may be only for a sentence or two; you may be only slightly off pitch; but it will happen to you again and again as it happens to every writer and speaker at all times. Let me give you a few horrible examples as a warning:

Here is a teacher who writes a book on *The How and Why of Life,* one of those "painless" disguised textbooks that are supposed to make children like biology. Cleverly she introduces little Bobby, who is forever asking questions, and his father, who is a doctor and knows all the answers. On page 5, to start the pair off on biology, Mother has twins. Bobby, who knows his cue, asks Father: "How did it happen that Mother had two babies instead of one?" And here is Daddy's immortal answer:

"All mammals which usually have one offspring at a time, occasionally have multiple births."

What happened here is obvious: the poor teacher-author got lost in textbook language and couldn't find her way back to plain English; so, working hard to "make it a story," she wound up with a husband who calls his wife a mammal.

Let's take another example. This is a choice bit from a radio talk a doctor gave one weekday afternoon to housewives. The topic was what to do with children who get sick. Listen:

> . . . Although I stressed organic disease, one must not lose sight of the early symptoms of behavior disorders, which are amenable to proper management under the guidance of your physician. But in addition to behavior problems *per se,* changes in behavior may themselves indicate organic disease. . . .

Do you understand what he means? Do you think the housewives understood? Do you think they will be able to tell a "behavior problem *per se*" when they see one?

But you may say that these outrages were committed by teachers and doctors; professional writers would never do such things. Let's see. How about advertising copy writers? Aren't they paid and specially trained to talk the language of the reader? Well, look at the following ad. It appeared in *Time* magazine under one of those deceptive captions that make you believe for a few seconds that you are reading news rather than an ad. Surely the writer must have tried to keep in tune with *Time's* editorial style. But did he? I reprint the ad with what appeared in a parallel column so that you can see for yourself:

(*Advertisement*)

HOTELS

The dining revolution which rationing has wrought since the beginning of the current war is mild indeed when compared with the typical Parker House banquet of pre-Civil War days. The contrast was dramatically highlighted recently by the unusual menu of a "Dinner for Twenty-four Gentlemen" given at the Parker House in 1857. Discovered in the archives of Boston's well-known Webster and Atlas National Bank, which is celebrating its 110th anniversary this year, the physical format of the menu is something the like of which has not been seen for many a year. And the abundance and variety of the following feast will not be seen on a hotel menu for many a month to come. . . .

SPORT

Big Bill Gonsalves, who works as a mechanic at the Worthington Pump Co. when he is not playing soccer, is a 200-lb. six-footer with a tremendous kick in his massive legs. One of soccer's hardest shots, he can boot a ball fast enough to break a man's hand. From 20 yards he has often broken the goal's netting. . . .

Now never mind, if you can, that we have here in four sentences a *revolution* that *dines* and is being compared with a *banquet*; a *recent* dinner given in *1857*; and a *physical format* that is *discovered* in the *archives*. Just look at the style of the ad and compare it with the snappy sports news that makes *Time* readers turn to this page. That ad writer knows his public even less than his grammar.

The next exhibit comes from a book entitled *Let the People Know*. It was written by a famous political writer and Nobel Prize winner as an answer to questions in the mind of John Citizen, the average American man-in-the-street. At least that's what the author thinks the book is; actually, he writes in the same style he used in two dozen other books John Citizen never bothered about. So when he wants to say that people don't know—he has said that in the title anyhow—he prattles along:

> THE DANGERS OF MISINFORMATION
>
> We are dealing here perhaps rather with a misapprehension as to the actual facts than with a confusion as to the use of terms, but the facts themselves are important in this connection because they bear upon our view as to the line of solution. The remedy which the nations apply for the solution or alleviation of the very real economic difficulties which face them, will depend upon the extent to which they are dominated by, or free from, these elementary confusions. . . .

Let me put it this way: "The remedy to apply for the solution or alleviation of the very real *literary* difficulties which face" the writer of these lines, "will depend upon the extent to which he is dominated by, or free from, his elementary confusions" as to the way John Citizen talks.

Of course, you may say that all this business about John Citizen is just a literary convention; books on current affairs are read by only a few thousand intellectuals, as everyone knows. *Let the People Know* was probably a title the publisher dreamed up; and "John Citizen, the average American man-in-the-street" doesn't read books by Nobel Prize winners but sports news and the funnies.

True; but there are things John Citizen has to read whether he wants to or not. One of these must items is his income tax instructions; and they are—or were—written like this:

> (3) *Substantial Underestimate of Estimated Tax.*—In the case of individuals other than farmers, if 80 percent of the tax (determined without regard to the credits for tax withheld on tax-free covenant bonds and for Income and Victory Tax withheld on wages) exceeds the estimated tax (increased by such credits), and in the case of farmers, if 66 2/3 percent of the tax (determined without regard to such credits) exceeds the estimated tax (increased by such credits), there shall be added to the tax an amount equal to such excess, or equal to 6 percent of the amount by which the tax so determined exceeds the estimated tax so increased, whichever is the lesser.

Next time you get around to taxpaying you will have to read and understand sentences like this; right now, you may just look at it for a while the way you would look at a dinosaur skeleton in a museum. As your guide, I can tell you that it contains 107 words, 21 prepositions, 11 past participles, and 8 places where you have to do some arithmetic. And just to save you a sleepless night, here is the gist of it: if you guess your tax too low, you'll have to pay a fine but they can't fine you more than 6 per cent of your error. Now have another look at our dinosaur before we go on to the next monster.

This one comes from a book on science for laymen; not a scientific treatise, mind you, but one of those patchwork volumes made from two dozen pieces by outstanding scientists and put together to give the unscientific bystander a quick overview. Here is a specimen from the editor's preface:

> The fatal legacy of science, as it is unfortunately interpreted in contemporary anthropomorphic culture, is the too frequent insistence that the symbols do themselves constitute a logically autonomous and self-sufficient sys-

> tem, and that in the syntactical structure of that system resides the logical reality that has formerly been supposed to subsist in the extra-linguistic entities symbolized by the system.

That's what happens if you start talking about "extra-linguistic entities"—which are, I suppose, things beyond words. Don't bother to figure this one out: it's hopeless. I confess that I only put it here to sell you once and for all on plain talk; and I do hope that by now your mouth waters for homely, simple language as it would for a nice chunk of Grandmother's oven-baked brown bread.

Plain talk is just as hard to find as good, old-fashioned bread. There is only one difference: you can walk into any store today and buy "enriched" bread whose vitamins have been scientifically restored; but if you want to restore the vitamins to your language, you have to get down to work and learn how to do it yourself.

Chapter II

LET'S START WITH CHINESE

IF YOU had a smattering of Chinese, you could teach yourself simple English in no time. You could apply the Chinese way of talking to your own language, and without much effort you would form the habit of terse, clear, picturesque talk.

But all you know about Chinese, I take it, is chow mein and chop suey, and you probably don't care much about adding to your Chinese vocabulary. Therefore—and because I don't know any Chinese either—we shall do the next best thing: we shall study Chinese from the outside, so to speak, just to get a rough idea of how it is put together. Even that will bring us a long way nearer plain English.

That may sound odd to you. Chinese, to you, is an exotic language, written in quaint Oriental characters and spoken in a sort of singsong. Besides, the Chinese can't pronounce *r* and say things like "velly ploud" instead of "very proud."

True, some of them do; it so happens that their language does not have the *r* sound. It's also true that the meaning of spoken Chinese words depends on musical "tones," which makes it hard for us to learn spoken Chinese. What's more, their writing is based not on the alphabet but on graphic symbols that stand for whole words, which again makes it hard for us to learn written Chinese. In other words, Chinese is hard to approach; it has a sort of Chinese Wall around it.

But if you look behind that wall, you find that Chinese is really simple. Think of other languages, and what makes them difficult: conjugations, declensions, irregular verbs, ablatives, subjunctives, aorists—nightmares that plague every student who sets out to learn French, German, Latin, Greek, not to speak of Russian or Sanskrit. I don't have to tell you that what makes a language difficult is grammar.

Chinese, however, is known as a "grammarless" tongue. The list of the things it does *not* have is amazing: it has no inflections, no cases, no persons, no genders, no numbers, no degrees, no tenses, no voices, no moods, no infinitives, no participles, no gerunds, no irregular verbs, and no articles. There are no words of more than one syllable, every word has only one form, and all you have to learn is how to put these one-syllable words in their proper order. To make it still easier for you, this proper order is the same as the usual order in English: subject, predicate, object.

You may wonder how it is possible to talk in such a language so that other people understand you; and maybe you think this must be the most primitive, uncivilized language of the world. It would be a common error: up to about fifty years ago all language experts agreed that Chinese is the "baby talk of mankind." They were wrong: it is the most grown-up talk in the world. It is the way people speak who started to simplify their language thousands of years ago and have kept at it ever since.

For, thanks to research, we know now that thousands of years ago the Chinese language had case endings, verb forms, and a whole arsenal of unpleasant grammar. It was a cumbersome, irregular, complicated mess, like most other languages. But the Chinese people, generation after generation, changed it into a streamlined, smooth-running machine for expressing ideas. This isn't just a figure of speech: the main principle of modern Chinese is exactly the same as that of modern machinery. It consists of standardized, prefabricated, functionally designed parts.

In other words, Chinese is an assembly-line language. All the words are stripped to their essential meaning and purpose, and put together in a fixed order. Word order is as all-important as the order of operations on the assembly line: if you line it up in any other way it doesn't work. For instance, take the famous sentence *Dog bites man* that is not news but becomes news when it is turned around to *Man bites dog.* Here, word order is as important in English as it is in Chinese: it makes all the difference. In classical Latin, however, if you want to tell about the dog biting a man, you have to say something like *He-the-dog bites him-the-man.* Now try to turn it around: *Him-the-man bites he-the-dog.* No difference whatsoever: still no news. You see, the ancient Romans hadn't found out yet about the assembly-line principle.

Let's look closer at this example. In Latin you have to talk about *He-the-dog* and *Him-the-man.* Why? Because the word and the case ending are fused together and you can't say *man* or *dog* without also saying *he* or *him,* whatever the case may be. The reason is that Latin, like other difficult languages, expresses almost all grammatical relationships by endings (suffixes), or sometimes by prefixes at the beginning of a word. The significant thing about these prefixes and suffixes—the grammarians call both of them affixes—is the syllable "fix." They are fixed, firmly attached, stuck. If you try to use word order—the word-assembly-line—they get in the way. What you get in the end is not the striking headline you were after but *Him-the-man bites he-the-dog.*

So what did the Chinese do after they had got hold of the assembly-line idea? Simple: they threw out all the affixes. It was the logical thing to do. Soon—that means in Chinese after many thousands of years—they got rid of everything that fills our grammar textbooks and were left with a few thousand little syllables and rules for putting them in order. Now, if they wanted to say *A man bites a dog* they said *Man bite dog;* for *Two men bite two dogs* they said *Two man bite two dog;* for *Two men bit two dogs, Two man finish bite two dog;* and so on all through the language.

That was long before the time of Confucius, 500 B.C. Ever since, no Chinese school child has been plagued by grammar. In fact, the Chinese never knew that there was such a thing as grammar until they heard about it from us. All their language teachers ever did was to sort out full and empty words and let it go at that.

Now you will ask, What are full and empty words? If you

look at words closely, the answer is easy. Full words say something, empty words do not. They are just there to tie the full words together—language tissue that is necessary but doesn't convey any meaning. If somebody started talking to you and said: "Besides, however, nevertheless, as it is, with regard to, inasmuch, hence, indeed, but . . ." you would look at him in amazement and think, When will he start saying something? Up to now, he used only empty words.

Possibly this one-and-only feature of Chinese grammar may seem pointless to you. But the Chinese knew how to use it. After they had successfully stripped their language of all the unnecessary affix underbrush, they naturally wanted to go further in the process of streamlining. So they discovered that they could do without many of the empty words, and out they went. Why should anyone say *A dog is an animal,* if the same idea can be expressed by *Dog*: *animal?* Articles have no place in an assembly-line language. Neither has the verb *to be* wherever it is just filling the space between subject and predicate.

But all this was just the first step in simplification. You have to think this thing through to really understand what it means. You have to imagine a language where there is a difference between full and empty words *but no other distinction between words.* The Chinese never heard about nouns, verbs, and adjectives. To them, a word is just a word, and you use it where it fits in and makes sense. If a Chinese says *Sun shine,* he may mean *sunshine,* or *The sun is shining,* or *The sun is bright and shiny.* Or, to be more exact, he doesn't mean any of these things, because his language doesn't work that way; he means that the *sun* (subject) has something to do with *shine* (predicate), and that's all. You may understand me better if I give two examples in English where a word has a meaning regardless of its grammatical function. If you say: "Got your hair cut?" you don't think or care whether the word *cut* is a noun, a verb, or an adjective. Neither does the fellow who had, or had not, his hair cut. Still, both of you know what you are talking about. In the same way, if you read a headline THE AXIS SPLIT, you don't care about the grammatical function of *split,* but you are not in doubt what it means. Now imagine, if you can, a language that consists only of words like *cut* or *split* in these examples, and you will get some notion about Chinese.

If you started to talk and write in such a language, you would soon notice that it forces you into plain talk by various means. Try, for instance, to use complex sentences, or qualifying clauses and phrases. You will find that Chinese makes it hard to be hard. Can you start a sentence like this: "Biting a dog, a man . . ."? You can't. You have to stick to the good old assembly-line word order and say: "A man bit a dog. Then he . . ." Or how about the passive voice: "A dog, bitten by a man . . ."? Not in Chinese. Back to the assembly line: "A man bit a dog. The dog . . ." So you see, fancy language doesn't work in Chinese. Suppose you give that famous news story the works and write a headline like this:

TRAMP'S DENTAL ATTACK ON
WESTCHESTER PEKINESE REPORTED

In Chinese you could use neither affixes nor the passive voice and you couldn't tack on *reported* at the end. You would have to start out with something like

THEY SAY TRAMP-MAN TOOTH-HIT
PEIPING-TYPE DOG IN WESTCHESTER

and in no time you would be back at the old

MAN BITES DOG

But even that is not all. Chinese does more to you than just simplify your constructions. It simplifies your ideas. In other languages, the affixes are a splendid means of getting away from reality into vague generalities and abstractions. For instance, in English you have the simple word *sign,* meaning "a mark." Now you add an affix to that word and you get *signify,* "to make a mark." Next you add another affix, and you arrive at *significant,* "making a mark." Now you add a prefix for a change, and you have *insignificant,* "making no mark." Finally you add another suffix, and you come out with *insignif-*

icance, "the making of no mark." What did you do? You took a simple noun, and made it successively into a verb, an adjective, another adjective, and again a noun. You have added no meaning but just four empty syllables. Now you can be serious and philosophic and talk about the *insignificance of man.* A Chinese would say something about *Man no mark.* So, while you give in to the temptations of English affixes and fill your talk with masses of empty syllables and words, he keeps his feet on the ground and says everything in the most concrete, specific words. He has to; there are no other words in Chinese.

Not only that, Chinese never loses the human touch. Remember that in Chinese you always have to express subject and predicate, otherwise the words make no sense. Also, there is no passive voice. Therefore, in Chinese, you have to say clearly Who did What. You cannot say things like *It is reported by reliable authorities . . .* You have to say *People I rely on say . . .*

If you think, however, that Chinese has no way of expressing abstract ideas, you are wrong. Remember, the Chinese were talking and writing about religion and philosophy long before our own civilization started. If they had no exact word for an abstraction, they used the concrete word, or words, that came nearest to the idea. So, naturally, instead of using words like *institutionalization* or *antiprogressivism,* as our thinkers do, they formed the habit of expressing ideas by metaphors, similes, and allegories, in short, by every known device for making a thing plain by comparing it with something else. This is the feature of Chinese that is almost impossible to explain without going into the language itself; it's the flavor, the overtones, that are usually lost in translation. However, you may get the idea if I tell you that Chinese is full of things like

> He who raises himself on tiptoe cannot stand firm; he who stretches his legs wide apart cannot walk.

or

> Do not wish to be rare like jade, or common like stone

And maybe you will understand why I have gone into all this and started a book on plain English with a chapter on Chinese, if you look at two passages I found on the same newspaper page. They are from two war communiqués. One is the United Nations communiqué: cold, abstract, impersonal, official. The other is the Chinese communiqué (translated from a broadcast in the Mandarin language): it is concrete, human, grimly touching. Somehow you get the feeling that the two communiqués are about different wars, ours about World War II and the Chinese about some other distant, medieval, heroic war. Yet it's the same war, all right; the same bombs, the same tanks. The difference is not between Tommies or doughboys and Chinese soldiers; it is between the English language and Mandarin Chinese.

Here are the two reports:

UNITED NATIONS

Enemy resistance in certain sectors of the Fifth Army front was strong, but further progress was made by our troops. The important road center of Teano was captured, and elsewhere on the front more ground offering good observation was taken.

The recent heavy rains are making movement very difficult in the coastal sector.

CHINESE

On October 25 our forces engaged the enemy in a fierce battle in the vicinity of Chiuchiwu. The enemy troops were driven off and the area of Chiuchiwu was taken by our troops.

With encouragement from the excellent results in killing the enemy, our forces bravely launched several more thrusts, and more of the enemy troops were killed. During that engagement, the enemy commanding officer of Siaofeng was killed by our forces.

The total number of the enemy soldiers and officers killed amounted to more than 1,300. That was only the number of corpses found in the field. The enemy remnants fled to Siaofeng in a chaotic manner. Our troops followed the victory and continued to attack.

You will feel the difference even better if you try to imagine what the Chinese communiqué was like in the original. It must have sounded somewhat like this:

> October 25. Our force meet enemy. Fierce battle near Chiuchiwu. Our force drive off enemy troop; take Chiuchiwu country.
>
> Kill enemy good work: courage to our force. Launch some more brave thrust. Kill more enemy troop . . .

And so on; you can figure out the rest for yourself.

I am sure you will admit at this point that Chinese is a simple language. But, you will say, what has all that to do with plain English? You are already wondering whether I am going to make you write sentences like *Kill enemy good work*; and you don't particularly care for being quaint.

Don't worry: this book is about plain talk, and I mean plain talk. All we are going to do with our new nodding acquaintance with Chinese is to keep its two main principles firmly in mind: first, get rid of empty words and syllables and, second, stick to the subject-predicate-object order. That's how the Chinese simplified their language, and that's how we can simplify ours. All the rest follows: simple sentences, concreteness, the human touch.

And now you can already start with your first

Exercise

Translate the following passage into English that sounds like Chinese:

> An indigenous American faith in the desirability and necessity of applying the democratic principle to the intellectual life continued to bulk large among the forces back of all the emphasis on popularizing knowledge. The lyrical faith in education as the best means of promoting equality of opportunity was a main cause for the increasing public responsibility for schools and for the vast expansion of other agencies for popularizing knowl

edge. The traditional argument that mass education was necessary for intelligent participation in political democracy and that it must extend beyond the common school was heard in discussions regarding high schools, libraries, and Chautauquas. The growing complexity of American life and the recognition that this imposed new burdens on democratic political machinery were additional arguments for spreading knowledge through every possible channel.

In this exercise you have to throw out affixes and empty words and rewrite the sentences in subject-predicate-object order. To find out what an affix is you have to look up the words in a dictionary that gives exact derivations. (The handiest dictionary for this is the *Concise Oxford Dictionary*.) Then take the basic word meanings, stripped of all affixes, and line them up in order. Finally, build simple English sentences from these elements: you will get a free translation of the original paragraph into Chinese-flavored English.

Here is the first sentence as a sample. First, the word roots listed in order:

Born—America—believe—wish—want—people—mind—life—stay—big—force—drive—people—know

Now let's make this into a sentence:

Born Americans believe they wish and want mind-life for the people; this belief stayed: a big force in the drive to make people know.

Do the rest of the paragraph in the same fashion.

(If you would rather skip this exercise to read on, turn to the next chapter. But don't forget to go back to it if you want to get out of this book everything that's in it.)

Chapter III

LISTEN TO PLAIN TALK

AFTER reading so much about Chinese, you may think that simplified language is a Chinese specialty. Of course, that isn't so. All peoples simplify their languages. Whenever scientists had a chance of comparing an old language with its modern offspring, they found that inflections and irregularities had been dropped in the course of the centuries. No wonder: nobody uses a lot of difficult grammar if he can help it. I am sure you know plenty of people who keep on speaking broken English all their lives simply because they have found out they can get along; in the same manner nations use broken languages because it's easier to talk that way. Chinese is simpler than most other languages only because the Chinese people happened to be earlier in the game; the difference is really in time.

Among the world's great languages, the runner-up to Chinese is English. It's simpler, more flexible, more practical than any other Western language because it has gone furthest in losing inflections and straightening out irregularities. We say today *named* for what was in Old English *genemnode*; and we say *had* for what was in Gothic *habaidedeima*. We have almost no inflections or irregularities left now; in other words, we are approaching the point Chinese reached some time before 500 B.C. You would think we might catch up with them in a few thousand years.

But this will never happen. We lost our chance in the race when we became a literate people. For languages change only in the mouths of illiterates; if you start to teach children the three R's you stop them from simplifying their parents' language. If all Gothic boys and girls had learned how to spell *habaidedeima* generation after generation, they would never have got it down to *had*; billions of written and printed *habaidedeimas* would have been in the way. You have to take a language with an alphabet and a written literature as is; if you want to change *theatre* into *theater* it takes decades of crusading. (The Chinese, of course, had the added advantage of never having used an alphabet but a system of word symbols; so they could streamline their words without changes in spelling. Chinese just doesn't spell.)

That does not mean, however, that a literary language does not change at all. It does; but the changes are not in grammar and spelling but in style and expression. English settled down to its present spelling and grammar around 1600; but the prose style of that time was very different from ours. It was elaborate and slow; ours is informal and fast. Read, for instance, this sentence from Milton's *Areopagitica*, written in 1644:

> For if we be sure we are in the right, and do not hold the truth guiltily, which becomes not, if we ourselves condemn not our own weak and frivolous teaching, and the people for an untaught and irreligious gadding rout, what can be more fair, than when a man judicious, learned, and of a conscience, for aught we know, as good as theirs that taught us what we know, shall not privily from house to house, which is more dangerous, but openly by writing publish to the world what his opinion is, what his reasons, and wherefore that which is now taught can not be sound.

This is beautiful; but the point here is that nowadays nobody writes like that. If one of our own literary people had written that passage, it would read somewhat like this:

> Supposedly we know and don't purposely suppress the truth, our education is neither inefficient nor irresponsible, and there is no rampant ignorance and irreligion. Consequently, whoever is intelligent, educated and pre-

sumably honest should in all fairness be allowed to publish his arguments against current doctrine.

The main difference between the two versions is that a modern writer feels unable to take a long breath like Milton. He thinks he must condense everything important into few words and short sentences, and leave out everything else; no modern reader would stand for Miltonian periods.

That is true. But our modern authors have jumped out of the frying pan into the fire; their sentences are faster than those of the Elizabethans but less readable. Milton, in all his stateliness, is simpler reading than most modern literary prose. Instead of simplifying our written language, we have made it more complex.

So, if we look for a recipe for modern plain English, we find ourselves in a peculiar spot: we could try to imitate seventeenth-century English, but that would sound impossibly old-fashioned; or we could try to approach some future "Chinese" English, but that would sound impossibly modernistic. We have to take our language as it is today and find some compromise solution.

But where is the problem? you say. Doesn't everybody know the trouble with difficult English is those big, five-dollar words? Can't we just use plain one-syllable or two-syllable words instead and there we are? Can't we find the vocabulary range of our audience and then use only the words they know?

Unfortunately, we can't. There is no way of saying, This man has a vocabulary of 10,000 words, that one has a vocabulary of 10,001 words and so on. And even if we could say that, we couldn't go on and say, The one word Man No. 2 knows but Man No. 1 *doesn't* know is *hirsute*; therefore we can use *hirsute* with Man No. 2 but not with Man No. 1. That's all very ridiculous; but it's the logical conclusion to what most people think about plain language. To them, it's simply a vocabulary problem.

It's no vocabulary problem at all. In the first place, everybody recognizes words he never uses in talking. That's why you can safely talk about *irreligion* to people who would never say *irreligion* in their lives. In the second place, everybody is able to understand an unfamiliar word if only the circumstances make clear what it means. If I said to you, out of a clear sky, "Barberiana," you wouldn't understand. It may mean a Latin-American dance, or anecdotes about the late Professor Roderick W. Barber, or whatever. But if you had passed the barbershop in Rockefeller Center, and had seen in the window an exhibit of shaving mugs, barber's basins, and paintings of people who are having their hair cut, with a big sign underneath: BARBERIANA, you wouldn't need an explanation. And now your vocabulary has 27,394 words instead of 27,393.

Anyway, if you ever tried to write within a limited vocabulary, you would know that it can't be done. There are always words you specially want to use, and other words you have to use. For instance, in the second chapter of this book I used the word *aorist*. Possibly you don't know what an aorist is; or maybe you have just a vague idea that it is something in Greek grammar you are glad you forgot. Splendid: that's exactly what I wanted you to know or guess about the word. I didn't use it for its precise meaning; I used it for the unpleasantness it stands for. If it had been fully familiar to you, it wouldn't have been as frightening as I meant it to be.

Or, to take another example, I used the word *affix* in Chapter II, and I am going to keep on using it throughout this book. In fact, I couldn't write this book without using the word *affix* because that's what much of it is about. You may not have heard it before; so I have tried to give you a good explanation, and I hope that by now *affix* is part of your vocabulary.

In other words, to limit one's speaking and writing vocabulary is unnecessary, on the one hand, and impossible, on the other. True, the big five-dollar words are stumbling blocks for your audience; but now, in the middle of the twentieth century, there is almost nothing you can intelligently speak or write about without using those key words. For instance, there wouldn't be much point in talking about our form of government without using the word *democracy*.

Well, then, you will say, if simplified grammar is out, and slow-paced sentences are out, and limited vocabulary is out, how *can* we simplify our prose style? How does anyone achieve plain talk anyhow?

For, strange as it may seem to you at this point, people talk plainly as long as they don't think about it. In conversation, without rehearsal or preparation, they somehow manage to express themselves so clearly that nobody asks for an explanation. How do they do it?

The solution to this puzzle is easy: they use big words, and a fast pace, and the ordinary rules of grammar, *but they give the other fellow time to understand.* They pause between sentences; they repeat themselves; they use filler words between the big important ones; they space their ideas. The secret of plain talk is in-between space.

That sounds simple; in fact, it *is* simple. Everyone does it every day. But when it comes to writing, or to formal speaking, we forget about the in-between space. It doesn't seem right to fill pages with filler words or repetition and that sort of thing doesn't go with oratory. So we compress and condense; we make one word out of three, and leave out ten more that seem irrelevant. They *are* irrelevant; but without them, your reader or listener has no time to understand the relevant words. You have to use small talk in between if you want your big talk to go over. What you say may be clear for anybody with average intelligence; but don't forget that you force that average-intelligent man to make an effort to follow you. Maybe he has other things on his mind; maybe he is tired; or maybe he simply is not interested enough to make that effort. If you fill in space, you won't add anything to what you say; but you will put your audience at ease.

It seems almost impossible to illustrate this point. No writer describes conversation as it really is; and we don't take shorthand notes of what we say to each other in our living rooms or on our porches. But it is necessary for the purpose of this book that you get an exact idea of colloquial prose. So I reprint here two rather long pieces that are as accurate reproductions of conversation as can be found. They are not perfect; but I hope they will give you the right idea.

The first excerpt is from a story by Dorothy Parker, entitled "Too Bad." Two gossiping women serve as a sort of Greek chorus, interpreting the story to the reader; and Dorothy Parker is remarkably successful in making gossip sound like gossip:

> "My dear," Mrs. Ames said to Mrs. Marshall, "don't you really think that there must have been some other woman?"
>
> "Oh, I simply couldn't think it was anything like that," said Mrs. Marshall. "Not Ernest Weldon. So devoted—home every night at half-past six, and such good company, and so jolly, and all. I don't see how there *could* have been."
>
> "Sometimes," observed Mrs. Ames, "those awfully jolly men at home are just the kind."
>
> "Yes, I know," Mrs. Marshall said. "But not Ernest Weldon. Why, I used to say to Jim, 'I never saw such a devoted husband in my life,' I said. Oh, not Ernest Weldon."
>
> "I don't suppose," began Mrs. Ames, and hesitated. "I don't suppose," she went on, intently pressing the bit of sodden lemon in her cup with her teaspoon, that Grace—that there was ever anyone—or anything like that?"
>
> "Oh, Heavens, no," cried Mrs. Marshall. "Grace Weldon just gave her whole life to that man. It was Ernest this and Ernest that every minute. I simply can't understand it. If there was one earthly reason—if they ever fought, or if Ernest drank, or anything like that. But they got along so beautifully together—why, it just seems as if they must have been crazy to go and do a thing like this. Well I can't begin to tell you how blue it's made me. It seems so awful!"
>
> "Yes," said Mrs. Ames, "it certainly is too bad."

The other bit of conversation is not gossip but talk about current affairs between men; and it is not fictional but real. It is from a transcript of *The People's Platform*, a radio discussion program in the form of an overheard dinner-table conversation. These broadcasts are unrehearsed and spontaneous. I think the transcripts are the nearest thing to actual-conversation shorthand notes that can be found. Of course, the broadcast dinner guests know they are on the air; but they talk to each other and not to their audience.

This particular program was about Russia. The chairman was Lyman Bryson; the guests, Walter Duranty, Louis Fischer, and Max Lerner. Listen:

> FISCHER: . . . Of course, when Churchill and Roosevelt meet . . . they inevitably discuss the Pacific which is such an important phase of the whole war, but . . .
>
> BRYSON: And to Russia also?
>
> FISCHER: And to Russia, of course! But the Russians have been invited to previous conferences where the Pacific was also discussed, but they were *not* invited to this conference and I think they were not invited to this conference because Russia is being discussed in terms of Russian demands and the Russians want to know the answers.
>
> LERNER: I don't know, Bryson, whether Fischer or Duranty, which of them is correct about this, but there's one observation I'd like to make about the whole thing and that is this seems to indicate what is to me the most serious problem in the relations of the Allies, and that is America and Britain are always meeting about something and Russia isn't meeting with them. There seems to have been developing a rift within the United Nations . . . we're becoming almost a house divided against itself. At least there is a danger that we may become a house divided or . . .
>
> FISCHER: Well, isn't it true, Lerner, that Stalin has been invited several times and has not seen fit or not been able to come?
>
> LERNER: I don't know, Fischer. I have been told that.
>
> FISCHER: Well, we have been told that officially and Roosevelt said only the other day at his press conference that he would have been glad to meet Stalin. . . .
>
> LERNER: Well, may I just say this and that is that just

this morning we had reports of an editorial published in a Russian semiofficial magazine asking for a meeting of the three powers. Now, it's very difficult to reconcile that with the statement that Stalin had repeatedly been invited to such a meeting and had not taken part.

FISCHER: Oh, he might have refused it in the past and sees the wisdom of it now.

LERNER: That's possible.

DURANTY: Yes. Well, you speak, Lerner, of a rift between Russia and the Western powers . . . has it grown up recently? Isn't it really more true that there has been concealed distrust and misunderstanding between Russia and the Western democracies ever since the foundation of the Soviet Republic and that actually today we are merely witnessing a progression of that and a continuation of it, and what's more . . .

LERNER: It's getting worse!

DURANTY: I say it's not getting much better because in many ways the situation is acute. For instance, this very question of the second front and other questions. I think on the whole it is probably getting better, but in a sense sharper at this time. And that, after all, many people in Germany and outside Germany have an interest in extending this squabble, or pretending it is a quarrel where it is not, perhaps even somewhat unconsciously.

LERNER: Yes, because I agree, Duranty, that this distrust is an old thing and one of the interesting things is that this distrust has not been destroyed by Russian bravery and Russian military accomplishment and by our cooperating with the Russians, our Lease-Lend. Distrust is rarely destroyed between nations and it seems to be really rechanneled . . . it's now seeking underground, subterranean methods of showing itself . . . in an enormous amount of rumormongering on both sides and the suspicions that the Russians have of us, in our tendency, as I say, to act with the British but not to act with the Russians so that I would suggest that one of the things for us as Americans . . . us Americans to think about is what can we do to . . . well, shall we say . . . destroy this distrust on our side?

FISCHER: Well, I think we can. . . . The first thing we can do is to try to understand why it is sharper today, as Duranty says, than it has been throughout Soviet history, and I think that the reason is . . . lies in the nature of this war. . . .

Now if you read these two conversation pieces carefully, you will notice how the speakers make themselves understood. They repeat phrases ("I don't suppose . . . I don't suppose" —" . . . they were not invited to this conference and I think they were not invited to this conference because . . ."); they correct themselves (". . . that Grace—that there was ever anyone . . ."—". . . whether Fischer or Duranty, which of them is correct . . ."—". . . the reason is . . . lies in the nature of this war. . . .") ; they repeat ideas in different words (" . . . a progression of that and a continuation of it . . ."—". . . our cooperating with the Russians, our Lease-Lend."); they even contradict their own statements ("I say it's not getting much better . . . I think on the whole it is probably getting better . . .").

Sometimes the speakers use sentences of Chinese simplicity ("It was Ernest this and Ernest that every minute."—"America and Britain are always meeting about something and Russia isn't meeting with them"). At other times they use old-fashioned slow-moving sentences—but with the difference that they don't say them in one breath but break them into pieces ("If there was one earthly reason—if they ever fought, or if Ernest drank, or anything like that. But they got along so beautifully together—"—". . . just this morning we had reports of an editorial published in a Russian semiofficial magazine asking for a meeting of the three powers. Now it's very difficult to reconcile that with the statement that Stalin had repeatedly been invited to such a meeting and had not taken part").

Important key words are being used where they seem necessary, but always with some illustration or rephrasing to drive the point home ("So devoted—home every night at half-past six, and such good company, and so jolly, and all."—". . . a rift within the United Nations . . . we're becoming almost a house divided against itself."—". . . it seems to be really re-channeled . . . it's now seeking underground, subterranean methods of showing itself . . .").

Everything is put in personal terms ("Why, I used to say to Jim . . ."—"I can't begin to tell you how blue it's made me."—". . . what is to me the most serious problem . . ."—". . . we have been told that . . ."—". . . I would suggest that one of the things for us as Americans . . . us Americans to think about . . .").

Filler words are freely strewn about ("Oh"—"yes"—"why"—"Heavens, no"—"well"—"of course"—"that is"—"well"—"now"—"oh"—"yes"—"I say"—"I think"—"well, shall we say"—"well").

And finally there is one element you can't see on the printed page: between the words and with them there are gestures and looks and intonations and pauses and silences.

So here we have the secret of plain conversational talk: it is not difficult ideas expressed in easy language, it is rather abstractions embedded in small talk. It is heavy stuff packed with excelsior. If you want to be better understood you don't have to leave out or change your important ideas; you just use more excelsior. It's as simple as that.

Exercise

Translate the following passage into conversational talk, as if it were spoken across a dinner table. Be sure to use all the ideas that are there, but provide space between them. Do not add any new ideas of your own.

> Perhaps the toughest job of thinking we have to do in this matter of European reconstruction is to realize that it can be achieved through nonpolitical instrumentalities. Reconstruction will not be politics; it will be engineering.
>
> It will be possible to operate Europe's primary economic plant directly, not through political controls. It is pos-

> sible to make bargains with cartels and trusts, with trade unions and co-operatives, with farm unions and professional societies, without sending a single *démarche* through a foreign ministry or memorandum through a Department of the Interior. For a year or more after the First World War many cities and districts in central and eastern Europe provided for their immediate needs while their paper governments issued decrees and proclamations that meant exactly nothing. So long as food can be procured, politicians are expendable. And so long as the Commission can provide the minimum supplies needed to sustain local life it can make trains run, and ships sail, and oil wells spout, and factory chimneys smoke.
>
> Why it will often have to deal directly with nonpolitical bodies should be fairly clear. Unless a totalitarian police power is to administer everything (and it is unthinkable that our armies should provide and subsidize such forces) there can be in the more chaotic parts of Europe no responsible and effective national political authority for a long time.

As a sample, here is my own conversational version of the first paragraph:

> Well, there is quite a tough job ahead . . . the toughest of them all, I think, as far as this matter of Europe—of European reconstruction is concerned. . . . Yes, the toughest job we have to do in this whole matter, and it's a job of thinking—of realizing how it can be done—how it will be done, I should say. . . . It will be done somehow, but not by politics. No, reconstruction in Europe won't be politics at all. . . . What I mean is this: it will all be nonpolitical. Nonpolitical bodies and agencies and bureaus—nonpolitical instrumentalities of all kinds. You see, it will be an engineering job. Like building a bridge, that's the way I look at it. . . . No politics whatsoever, mind you, just plain nonpolitical engineering. . . . Yes, that's the way you have to realize—to visualize this reconstruction job."

Now do the rest of the passage in the same manner.

Chapter IV

SENTENCES COME FIRST

PERHAPS by now you have a general idea of what simplified language looks like and how people go about making themselves understood in conversation. Plain talk is mainly a question of language structure and of spacing your ideas. Now let's get down to work and learn how to do this.

We shall start with sentences, for the simple reason that language consists of sentences. Most people would say offhand that language consists of words rather than sentences; but that's looking at it the wrong way. We do not speak by forming one sentence after another from words we have stocked somewhere back in our brains: we try to say what we have in mind and tell it in sentences. This obvious fact is confirmed by what we know about the language of primitive peoples, where the issue is not confused by grammar and dictionary knowledge. Here is, for instance, what Frank C. Laubach, the famous teacher of illiterates, tells about the Maranaw language: "When we tried to write the words we heard, nobody could tell us where one word began and another ended! If I asked Pambaya, 'What is the Maranaw word for *go*?' he did not know. But if I asked how to say 'Where are you going?' he answered at once, 'Andakasoong.' By many trials and errors we discovered that *anda* was *where, ka* was *you,* and *soong* was *go*—'Where you go?' "

Of course, English has advanced far beyond Maranaw; but the principle still holds that words are discovered by taking sentences apart, and that the units by which we express ideas are sentences rather than words. So, to learn how to say things simply, we have to start by studying sentences.

Now, what is a sentence? Let's take our definition from Fowler's *Dictionary of Modern English Usage.* (This is the most famous elbow book for English writers. Incidentally, it's fun to read.) "A sentence means a set of words complete in itself, having either expressed or understood in it a subject and a predicate, and conveying a statement or question or command or exclamation." Fowler adds, and this is important: "Two sentences (not one): *You commanded and I obeyed.*" Naturally, it would also be two sentences if you wrote: "*You commanded; I obeyed.*"

So you see that ordinarily a sentence expresses one thought and you need two sentences to express two thoughts. You can, however, work one sentence into another in place of a noun or adjective or adverb: it then becomes a clause and the other sentence a complex sentence. You can also work more ideas into a sentence by putting in more phrases or words.

Every word you set into the framework of a sentence has to be fitted into its pattern; it has to be tied in with invisible strings. In a simple sentence like *Man bites dog* there is one such string between *man* and *bites* and another between *bites* and *dog,* and that's all there is to the sentence pattern. But if a sentence goes beyond the subject-predicate-object type, it is liable to become a net of crisscrossing strings that have to be unraveled before we can understand what it says.

Take for instance this sentence from a recent book on Russia:

> Here is Edmund Burke, the eminent British Liberal, than whom no European statesman was more horrified by the outrages of the French Revolution.

As you see, the clause is tied to the main sentence by the word *whom,* from which an invisible string leads to *Burke,* five words back. To reach *whom,* however, we have to jump over *than* which in turn is tied to *more horrified,* five words ahead. In short, the sentence is a tangle and should have been revised to read:

> No other European statesman was more horrified by the outrages of the French Revolution than Edmund Burke, the eminent British Liberal.

Old-fashioned grammarians would point out that the main idea should never have been expressed in the subordinate clause; but that rule of thumb is pure superstition. The important thing is that the ties within the sentence should not run in different directions but straightforward so that the reader can read along. Here is a good example of what I mean (from the theater section of the *New Yorker*):

> In an otherwise empty week, we might as well give the play our attention, if only as an almost perfect example of how a script of no conceivable merit manages to get cast, rehearsed and finally produced at some expense without anybody connected with it being aware that the whole enterprise is a violent and batty flight in the face of providence. In this case, of course, Mr. Paley has put on his own work, but it still seems incredible that nobody once took him aside and explained that even in these queer times there is no reliable metropolitan audience for amateur theatricals.

These sentences are not hard to read in spite of their complexity. The trouble is, you have to be a skillful writer to turn this trick. Ordinarily, a sentence will get tangled up as soon as you start filling it up with ideas. If you remember what I said in the last chapter about spacing ideas, you will understand that the best plan is to write short sentences so that the reader, or listener, gets enough chances for breathing spells and doesn't get caught in invisible strings between words.

That sounds elementary; and you may wonder why you find so many long sentences in books, magazines, and newspapers. The explanation, to the best of my knowledge, is simply that those sentences are written, not to make it easy for the reader, but to ensnare him, catch him like a fly on flypaper, or buttonhole him to attention. There are reasons for doing this; sometimes even good reasons. The most commonplace is the let-me-finish-my-sentence feeling of the raconteur, the storyteller who doesn't want to let go of his audience. Here is a simple example of the raconteur-sentence from a story by Damon Runyon:

> Well, Charley takes the dice and turns to a little guy in a derby hat who is standing next to him scrooching back so Charley will not notice him, and Charley lifts the derby hat off the little guy's head, and rattles the dice in his hand and chucks them into the hat and goes "Hah!" like crap shooters always do when they are rolling the dice.

Such a sentence is very loosely tied together; besides, it is really two sentences joined by *and.* If we want to disentangle it, we can rewrite it easily:

> Well, Charley takes the dice. He turns to a little guy in a derby hat who is standing next to him scrooching back so Charley will not notice him. Charley lifts the derby hat off the little guy's head, rattles the dice in his hand, chucks them into the hat and goes "Hah!" Crapshooters always do that when they are rolling the dice.

Now listen to a charming literary raconteur, Alexander Woollcott:

> If this report were to be published in its own England, I would have to cross my fingers in a little foreword explaining that all the characters were fictitious—which stern requirement of the British libel law would embarrass me slightly because none of the characters is fictitious, and the story—told to Katharine Cornell by Clemence Dane and by Katharine Cornell to me—chronicles what, to the best of my knowledge and belief, actually befell a young English physician whom I shall call Alvan Barach, because that does not happen to be his name.

This is already more difficult to unravel, but here we go:

> If this report were to be published in its own England, I would have to cross my fingers in a little foreword explaining that all the characters were fictitious; and that stern requirement of the British libel law would embarrass me slightly because none of the characters *is* fictitious. The story was told by Clemence Dane to Katharine Cornell and by Katharine Cornell to me: it chronicles

what, to the best of my knowledge and belief, actually befell a young English physician. I shall call him Alvan Barach because that does *not* happen to be his name.

Similar in purpose to the raconteur-sentence is the newspaper lead-sentence. The reporter, following a hoary rule of journalism, tries to get everything important into the first sentence so that the reader whose eyes happen to get caught by the headline, starts reading and cannot stop until he knows the gist of the story. This system gets the news down the reader's throat whether he wants it or not, but it makes newspaper reading a very unpleasant job. This is what you are likely to get with your breakfast:

> The Germans have completed a mine belt three miles wide along the west coast of Jutland in Denmark as part of their invasion defenses, and preparations to meet the Anglo-American onslaught from the west have been reviewed in Berlin where Adolf Hitler and Field Marshal Gen. Wilhelm Keitel, chief of staff to the Supreme Command, met Field Marshal Gen. Karl von Rundstedt, commander of the Wehrmacht in France.

Or, translated from tapeworm English into plain language:

> The Germans have completed a mine belt three miles wide along the west coast of Jutland in Denmark. This is part of their invasion defenses. Adolf Hitler, Field Marshal Gen. Wilhelm Keitel (chief of staff to the Supreme Command), and Field Marshal Gen. Karl von Rundstedt (commander of the Wehrmacht in France) met in Berlin. They reviewed preparations to meet the Anglo-American onslaught from the west.

Scientists, eager to win their argument, also often buttonhole their readers with long sentences. For instance:

> Learning a language need not be dull, if we fortify our efforts by scientific curiosity about the relative defects and merits of the language we are studying, about its relation to other languages which people speak, and about the

> social agencies which have affected its growth or about circumstances which have molded its character in the course of history.

Maybe the argument would sound even more convincing like this:

> Learning a language need not be dull. We can fortify our efforts by scientific curiosity about the language we are studying: What are its relative defects and merits? How is it related to other languages people speak? What social agencies have affected its growth? What circumstances have molded its character in the course of history?

The most notorious long-sentence writers are the lawyers. The reason is again similar: they won't let the reader escape. Behind each interminable legal sentence seems to be the idea that all citizens will turn into criminals as soon as they find a loophole in the law; if a sentence ends before everything is said, they will stop reading right there and jump to the chance of breaking the rule that follows after the period.

Well, that's questionable psychological doctrine; what is certain is that legal language is hard even on lawyers. Here is a mild example:

> Sick leave shall be granted to employees when they are incapacitated for the performance of their duties by sickness, injury, or pregnancy and confinement, or for medical, dental or optical examination or treatment, or when a member of the immediate family of the employee is affected with a contagious disease and requires the care and attendance of the employee, or when, through exposure to contagious disease, the presence of the employee at his post of duty would jeopardize the health of others.

Now I cannot believe that sick leaves would greatly increase or decrease if this were formulated as follows:

> Employees shall be granted sick leaves for these four reasons:

(1) They cannot work because of sickness, injury, or pregnancy and confinement;

(2) They need medical, dental or optical treatment;

(3) A member of their immediate family is affected with a contagious disease and needs their care and attendance;

(4) Their presence at their post of duty would jeopardize the health of others through exposure to contagious disease.

Finally, long sentences can be used for artistic reasons. Marcel Proust, the great French writer, built his novels from never-ending sentences—with the effect that the reader feels magically transposed into a world of dreamy memories and intense feelings. This is hard to describe; but you may want to taste just one sentence:

> But now, like a confirmed invalid whom, all of a sudden, a change of air and surroundings, or a new course of treatment, or, as sometimes happens, an organic change in himself, spontaneous and unaccountable, seems to have so far recovered from his malady that he begins to envisage the possibility, hitherto beyond all hope, of starting to lead—and better late than never—a wholly different life, Swann found in himself, in the memory of the phrase that he had heard, in certain other sonatas that he had made people play over to him, to see whether he might not, perhaps, discover his phrase among them, the presence of one of those invisible realities in which he had ceased to believe, but to which, as though the music had had upon the moral barrenness from which he was suffering a sort of recreative influence, he was conscious once again of a desire, almost, indeed, of the power to consecrate his life.

I am not going to translate this sentence into simple prose, first, because, in cold print, this would look like an insult to Proust's memory and, second, because this will be an excellent exercise for you after you finish this chapter. I am afraid it will keep you busy for a while.

Meanwhile you may ask, what is the moral of all this? Shall we write nothing but short, simple sentences? Shall we dissect every long sentence we find? Is there any rule?

No, there is no rule. But there are scientific facts. Sentence length has been measured and tested. We know today what average Americans read with ease, and what sentence length will fit an audience with a given reading skill. So you get not a rule but a set of standards.

To understand the table that follows, remember two things:

First, sentence length is measured in words because they are the easiest units to count: you just count everything that is separated by white space on the page. But don't forget that you might just as well count syllables, which would give you a more exact idea of sentence length: a sentence of twenty one-syllable words would then appear shorter than a sentence of ten one-syllable words and six two-syllable words. Keep that in mind while counting words.

Second, remember Fowler's definition of a sentence. Count two sentences where there are two, even if there is no period between them but only a semicolon or colon. But don't bother about sorting out sentences with conjunctions between them: the difference is not worth the added effort.

Now look at the table:

AVERAGE SENTENCE LENGTH IN WORDS

VERY EASY	8 or less
EASY	11
FAIRLY EASY	14
STANDARD	17
FAIRLY DIFFICULT	21
DIFFICULT	25
VERY DIFFICULT	29 or more

Just what EASY and DIFFICULT means on this table, I shall explain in detail later. For the moment, notice that an average reader will have no trouble with an average sentence of 17 words. (In a book or article, shorter sentences will, of course, cancel out the longer ones.) Easy prose is often written in 8-word sentences or so. Such writing consists mostly of dialogue and, as everybody knows, a book with a lot of dialogue is easy to read. On the upper half of the scale, literary English runs to about 20 words a sentence, and scientific English to about 30 words. The average sentence in this book has 18 words.

So, if you want to rewrite or edit something for people who are just about average, measure it against the 17-word standard. If the sentences are longer, look for the joints in their construction and break them into smaller pieces until they are of the right average length.

As an

EXERCISE

as I said before, you may try your hand at the Proust passage. If this seems too forbidding, here is another newspaper lead-sentence for you to dissect:

> Because Allied postwar planning groups like the United Nations Relief and Rehabilitation Administration realize the chaotic conditions with which they will be confronted by legally unidentifiable persons following the German collapse, leading British and American archivists are here on a tour that will probably lead to redefinition within the framework of military necessity of a system of handling damaged or newly occupied properties, it was learned today.

Rewrite this in easy 11-word sentences.

Chapter V

GADGETS OF LANGUAGE

NOW that we know what to do about sentences, the next question is, of course, what kind of words to put in them. This is the main topic of all books on how to write and I cannot start this chapter better than by quoting the beginning of the best of the lot, Fowler's *The King's English* (where you can study systematically what is arranged by the alphabet in his *Dictionary of Modern English Usage*): "Any one who wishes to become a good writer should endeavour, before he allows himself to be tempted by the more showy qualities, to be direct, simple, brief, vigorous, and lucid. This general principle may be translated into practical rules in the domain of vocabulary as follows:—

Prefer the familiar word to the far-fetched.

Prefer the concrete word to the abstract.

Prefer the single word to the circumlocution.

Prefer the short word to the long.

Prefer the Saxon word to the Romance.

These rules are given roughly in order of merit; the last i also the least."

Sir Arthur Quiller-Couch, in his Cambridge lectures *On th Art of Writing*, adds one more rule: "Generally use transitiv verbs, that strike their object; and use them in the activ voice, eschewing the stationary passive, with its little auxiliar *is's* and *was's,* and its participles getting into the light of you adjectives, which should be few. For, as a rough law, by hi use of the straight verb and by his economy of adjectives yo can tell a man's style, if it be masculine or neuter, writing o 'composition'."

This is, in a nutshell, the best advice you can get anywhere. If you look at these rules closely, you will find that those about short and Saxon words are admittedly not worth much, and that Quiller-Couch's rule starts with an arbitrary preference for transitive verbs—as if *lay* were a better word than *lie*. You will also see that the first rule about familiar words depends not on your own familiarity with words but on your reader's, which is hard to guess. And you will realize that the excellent rule about the single word being better than the circumlocution is unnecessary as long as you stick to what you learned from the last chapter and use as few words as possible in your sentences.

This leaves us with Fowler's second rule: "Prefer the concrete word to the abstract." Very good. Plain talk, as we all know, consists of concrete words; that's practically a definition of it. But which words are concrete and which abstract? You think you know? Well, is *apple* a concrete word? Of course, you say: you can look at apples, smell them, touch them, eat them. But how about the concept *apple*? Isn't it true that the word *apple* also stands for what all the apples in the world have in common, for their "appleness"? Isn't that abstract? How can you tell about any word whether it is abstract or concrete?

Actually, it is a question of meaning and of degree. Some words, like *democracy*, can safely be called abstract since they are used chiefly with abstract meaning; others, like *apple*, are felt to be concrete because they usually apply to concrete objects. It is possible—I have done it once—to draw up a long list of the most common abstract words and then check the abstractness of writing by the proportion of those words. But this is a cumbersome thing to do. You can get the same result in a far quicker and easier way if you count the language gadgets.

For language consists of two parts: the things we say and the machinery by which we say them. To express our thoughts, as we have seen, we use sentences; and we cannot express a thought by any single word unless it is able to do the work of a sentence if necessary. So we can tell the meaningful words apart from the mere language machinery by the sentence test: if a word can form a sentence, it refers to something outside language; if it cannot, it is just a language gadget. This has nothing to do with abstractness and concreteness: it is a linguistic difference. For instance, the abstract word *sin* can be used as a sentence, as in the famous answer to the question "What was the sermon about?" But the next question, "What did the preacher say?" had to be answered by a whole sentence: "He was against it." "*Against*" by itself wouldn't do as an answer; neither would *dis-* for "He disapproved of it." That's because *against* and *dis-* are examples of language gadgets; they have no meaning except combined with meaningful words in a sentence.

Now, the point of all this is that difficult, complex, abstract language is cluttered up with gadgets. If we stick to this purely linguistic test, we can measure difficulty by counting gadgets, and we can simplify our speech and writing by throwing them out.

Language gadgets, as you have seen, are of two kinds: words by themselves, like *against,* and parts of words (affixes), like *dis-*. The more harmful of the two for plain talk are the affixes, since the reader or hearer cannot understand what the gadget does to the sentence before he has disentangled it from the word it is attached to. Each affix burdens his mind with two jobs: first, he has to split up the word into its parts and, second, he has to rebuild the sentence from these parts. To do this does not even take a split second, of course; but it adds up.

If you want to measure word difficulty, therefore, you have to count affixes. Here is what you do: You count every affix you find in your text, every prefix, suffix, or inflectional ending, with the exception of -s at the end of a word, -en in *children, oxen* etc., and -d or -t in *could, did, had, might, ought, should, stood, went, would.* Some words have two affixes, like *dis-ap-prove,* some have three, like *dis-ap-prov-ing* Some seem to have nothing but affixes like *philo-soph-y*; discount one in such words. When you have finished counting figure out how many affixes there are per 100 words; or, of course, you can take a 100-word sample to begin with. Then you can check the result against this table:

NUMBER OF AFFIXES PER 100 WORDS

VERY EASY	22 or less
EASY	26
FAIRLY EASY	31
STANDARD	37
FAIRLY DIFFICULT	42
DIFFICULT	46
VERY DIFFICULT	54 or more

Again, for the time being, the average-reader standard of 37 is most important for you to know. The best example of VERY EASY prose (about 20 affixes per 100 words) is the King James Version of the Bible; literary writing tends to be FAIRLY DIFFICULT; scientific prose is VERY DIFFICULT. This book has on the average 33 affixes per 100 words.

To simplify a given passage, count first the number of affixes; then replace affix words systematically by root words, or at least by words with fewer affixes, until you arrive at the level you want to reach. The translating job is sometimes difficult and a dictionary with simple definitions will help. There are two dictionaries of this type on the market: one is the *Thorndike Century Senior Dictionary,* which defines words for high-school students; the other is *The New Method English Dictionary* by Michael West, which explains words to foreigners in a 2,000-word definition vocabulary. (A third one, Ogden's *General Basic English Dictionary,* is not recommended for this purpose.) Using Thorndike or West, however, is only a makeshift until somebody compiles a real simplifier's dictionary. Incidentally, both are useless for spotting affixes: the handiest tool for this, as I said before, is the *Concise Oxford Dictionary.*

Let me show you how it is done on a passage from *Reflections on the Revolution of Our Time* by Harold J. Laski. Laski, a leading British Socialist, writes well, and his topic is exciting; but unfortunately, he is a professor by trade and his language is pure academic jargon. Here is a key passage that seems worth translating into plain English:

> What is the essence of fascism? It is the outcome of capitalism in decay. It is the retort of the propertied interests to a democracy which seeks to transcend the relations of production implied in a capitalist society. But it is not merely the annihilation of democracy. It is also the use of nationalist feeling to justify a policy of foreign adventure in the hope, thereby, of redressing the grievances which are the index to capitalist decay. Wherever fascism has been successful, it has been built upon a protest by the business interests against the increased demands of the workers. To make that protest effective, the business interests have, in effect, concluded an alliance with some outstanding *condottiere* and his mercenaries who have agreed to suppress the workers' power in exchange for the possession of the state. But as soon as the condottiere has seized the state, he has invariably discovered that he cannot merely restore the classic outlines of capitalism and leave it there. Not only has his own army expectations. Having identified himself with the state, he has to use it to solve the problems through the existence of which he has been able to arrive at power. He has no real doctrine except his passionate desire to remain in authority. His test of good is the purely pragmatic test of success. And he finds invariably that success means using the state's power over the nation partly to coerce and partly to cajole it into acquiescence in his rule. That acquiescence is the sole purpose of, and the sole justification for, the methods that he uses. The only values he considers are those which seem likely to contribute to his success.

Now this has 56 affixes per 100 words and rates VERY DIFFICULT. The following translation has 32 and should read fairly easily:

> What makes fascism? It comes from capitalism in decay. It is the rich people's answer when democracy tries to go beyond the capitalist way of running production. But it does not stop at wiping out democracy. It also plays on the people's love for their country to put over dangerous

plans against other countries and so, they hope, to set right the wrongs capitalism in decay brings about. Wherever fascism has been successful, it has been helped at the start by businessmen trying to keep the workers from getting more. To do this, the businessmen have, in fact, joined up with some outstanding gang leader and his hired soldiers who have made a bargain to put down the workers' power and become owners of the state in return. But as soon as the gang leader has seized the state, he has always found that he cannot just bring back the standard forms of capitalism and leave it there. Not only does his own army wait for rewards. Now that he and the state are the same, he has to use it to solve the problems that made the businessmen put him in power. He has no beliefs except his strong wish to stay in power. His test of good is the test of success. And he always finds that success means using state-power to force or coax the people to yield to his rule. This is the sole purpose or reason for his methods. Useful to him is only what seems likely to add to his success.

You will notice that some of the key words have been left ntouched, like *fascism, capitalism, democracy, production.* ther affix words, like *decay, problem, success, methods,* did ot seem worth translating since they are easy to understand r every reader and would be hard to replace in this passage. emember that whenever you try to limit your vocabulary gidly, you become artificial and maybe un-English. If you ant to achieve plain talk, you have to avoid that mistake.

Another feature of the translation is that it is much shorter, ot only in syllables but also in words. Ordinarily, if you relace affix words by root words, you will have to use more ords. But it so happens that there is a lot of deadwood in is type of academic jargon that naturally falls by the wayde once you start rewriting. *He has no real doctrine* becomes *e has no beliefs,* and *the methods that he uses, his methods.*

I admit that it is not easy to write about economics or olitical science in easy language. Gifted writers are rare in this field; and a truly readable book like Bernard Shaw's *Intelligent Woman's Guide to Socialism and Capitalism* is a great exception. Let me quote to you, as contrast, how Shaw begins his "Appendix instead of a bibliography":

> This book is so long that I can hardly think that any woman will want to read much more about Socialism and Capitalism for some time. Besides, a bibliography is supposed to be an acknowledgment by the author of the books from which his own book was compiled. Now this book is not a compilation: it is all out of my own head. It was started by a lady asking me to write her a letter explaining Socialism. I thought of referring her to the hundreds of books which have been written on the subject; but the difficulty was that they were nearly all written in an academic jargon which, though easy and agreeable to students of economics, politics, philosophy and sociology generally, is unbearably dry, meaning unreadable, to women not so specialized. And then, all these books are addressed to men. You might read a score of them without ever discovering that such a creature as a woman had ever existed. In fairness let me add that you might read a good many of them without discovering that such a thing as a man ever existed. So I had to do it all over again in my own way and yours. And though there were piles of books about Socialism, and an enormous book about Capitalism by Karl Marx, not one of them answered the simple question, "What is Socialism?" The other simple question, "What is Capital?" was smothered in a mass of hopelessly wrong answers, the right one having hit on (as far as my reading goes) only once, and that was by the British economist Stanley Jevons when he remarked casually that capital is spare money. I made a note of that.

This is splendid writing, excellently readable for people like you and me. (It has 38 affixes per 100 words.) It just so happens that Shaw seems unable to write like this:

> The extensiveness of the present volume is such that it appears almost inconceivable that female readers should desire to prolong the study of Socialism and Capitalism for an additional period of time. This circumstance apart, a bibliography traditionally is supposed to serve as an acknowledgment offered by the author of the original sources that contributed to the genesis of his compilation. In contrast, however, to this usually followed procedure, the present volume differs radically from a compilation inasmuch as it was solely and entirely conceived and executed by the author himself. . . .

And so on. Translating normal English into affix English s easy; with the help of Roget's *Thesaurus* it's no work at ll. Moral: if you want to write plain English, don't use your Roget.

Exercise

Translate into Fairly Easy English (30 affixes per 100 words) the following passage from Laski:

> All government arises because men move in opposed ways to their objectives; no one but an anarchist would deny that its existence is, under any circumstances we can foresee, a necessary condition of peaceful social relations. But the argument that, especially in the economic sphere, we are over-governed, is not one with which it is easy to have patience. Less government only means more liberty in a society about the foundations of which men are agreed and in which adequate economic security is general; in a society where there is grave divergence of view about those foundations, and where there is the economic insecurity exemplified by mass-unemployment, it means liberty only for those who control the sources of economic power.

Chapter VI

THE GRAMMAR OF GOSSIP

TIME magazine prides itself that "our subscribers car understand the event in terms of the personality whc caused it. (Joe Stalin drinks his vodka straight. Admira Turner of the Central Pacific delights in growing roses. Ai Marshal Harris' men love him because he is "so bloody in human.")"

I wonder whether personalities really cause events an whether *Time* readers really understand the event bette because they are told about Stalin's vodka and Turner's roses But there is no doubt about one thing: human interest make for easier reading. Scientific tests have shown that people ar better at reading about other people than about anything else

Why is this so? Probably because man knows nothing so wel as man. His thinking and his language started out as simpl talk about what he and people around him were doing; an primitive man did not doubt that there was a person behin every event and behind every tree and mountain. Our moder languages, of course, have gone a long way toward abstractior but most of them still keep male and female genders for nam of things, and in German, for instance, the answer to th question "Where is my coat?" is: "He hangs in the closet."

So it seems to be naturally easier to read and understan *Stalin drinks vodka* than *Vodka contains alcohol.* To use on more my comparison between language and a machine shc where thoughts are prepared for the trade: think of yo entering such an empty shop and being baffled by it, and your relief when you at last find somebody to guide you. Th is what the name of a person in a sentence does to the reade

Therefore, after you have shortened your sentence and hrown out bothersome affixes, you have to do one more thing o make yourself well understood: you have to keep talking ibout people.

How can you do this, you ask. Many of the things you have o talk and write about just don't have any human interest; 'ou cannot properly discuss the situation on the stock market y telling stories about two Irishmen. The human touch in lain talk is not a question of language, you say, but of subect matter.

If you look closely at the way the human element is used n speech and writing, you will find that this is not so. People ome up in our sentences and paragraphs not only when we re gossiping but in discussions of everything under the sun. *Time* magazine, whose journalistic formula is built upon uman interest, is of course full of good examples. Here is ow various techniques are used for various subjects in a andom issue:

The classic newspaper device, the eyewitness report, is used or a war story:

> It was three days after the major part of the battle had ended and we were out a few miles from the island patrolling our little sector of the ocean, swinging back and forth in huge figures of eight. The noise and colors of battle were gone. The bombing had ceased and the big guns on the ships were silent.
>
> Now there was only a little smoke on the island and though we could see occasional puffs from the guns of the one destroyer which was still firing, the sound didn't carry to us. . . . A few of us were standing by the rail thinking our own thoughts when someone called attention to some objects in the water. . . . There were three of them, a hundred yards or more apart, and as we came closer we could see that they were men and that they were dead . . .

The interview technique is used for a bit of foreign news:

Everyone in Helsinki tells me that the Finnish food situation is now substantially better than it was twelve months ago. . . . As far as most ordinary Finns can see both on the front and in the rear, Finland is a defeated country in which wartime life is difficult but by no means intolerable.

The impression of most observers in Helsinki whom I have talked to is—in any case the Government should not close the doors for further negotiations with the Russians, but should try to get better terms than those which are now being discussed. Most Finns want peace under conditions which would assure Finland liberty and independence, but many doubt whether the present Russian proposals guarantee these to Finland.

A local story from New York is presented in the thriller-fictior manner:

At 4.50 a.m. the elevator signal buzzed in Internationa House, the massive 13-story lodging place built by Johr D. Rockefeller for foreign students. The elevator mar had a blind right eye, but as he stopped the car h turned to look at his lone passenger. She was Valsa Ann Matthai, 21, a pretty Indian girl from Bombay, a Colum bia University student. She was not wearing the India sari pulled over her hair, but a bright kerchief; and a she walked out of the empty, lighted lobby, the operato noticed she wore a tan polo coat, dark slacks, and spoi shoes. She had no bag. The street lights along Riversid Drive made pale yellow pools on the drifted snow, bu beyond, Grant's Tomb and the park sloping down to th Hudson River were lost in gloom. That was the mornin of March 20.

A speech is reported so that the reader never forgets th person who is talking:

The U.S. heard some plain talk last week on reco version. It came from War Mobilization Director Jam F. Byrnes in a speech before the Academy of Politic

Science in Manhattan. His most significant point: the harsh realities are at hand; big war plants are going to close down; in the next 20 months war production will be cut back some $16,750,000,000 at least; another $1,402,-000,000 will be slashed from the spare parts programs of the Army & Navy by the end of this year. Then Assistant President Byrnes warned:

"The Government must take a firm stand and close plants no longer needed in the war effort. From civic groups and from men in public office, there will come the cry: 'Woodman, spare the plant!' But we must realize that Santa Claus has gone."

Then Jimmy Byrnes came to grips with the question of dismissal pay for war workers . . .

A dramatic story like a Congressional committee hearing is written up as stage drama:

At committee hearings the people's representatives can give the admirals some uneasy moments.

One of these moments came when Vermont's Representative Charles A. Plumley found an item of $7,000,000 to build a stadium at Annapolis. That did not seem to Mr. Plumley to be essential to the war. Ernie King's deputy, Vice Admiral Frederick J. Horne (not the least of whose qualifications is his ability to get along with Congress) quickly admitted that the item should not have been put in the bill. "The bureau chiefs are here, and I think you are going to give them a bad quarter of an hour," said wry Admiral Horne.

For Mississippi's Jamie Whitten that dodge was not enough to excuse plushy requests for appropriations. Said he: "We just had Admiral King in here, and Admiral King says: 'I have to pass it right back to Admiral Horne'; now we have Admiral Horne here and he says 'I have to depend on the bureau chiefs,' and then the bureau chief says 'I have to depend on the men under me,' and it goes right down to the fellow who is at the Academy and wanted the stadium." Out went the stadium. Declared Jamie Whitten: "It takes a mighty small item to make you suspicious of the big items."

And, of course, no issue of *Time* is without its biographical profile, skillfully woven together out of little anecdotes:

> All his life Jack Curtin, 59, had never felt the need to see the non-Australian world. Years ago, Vance Marshall, an Australian laborite now living in London, visited Jack in Perth. "I'm on my way to England," Marshall said . . . "Australia's in the backwash. It's back of beyond of even the fringe of things that matter. I want to be where history is written."
>
> Jack reached for his well-worn hat, suggested a "walkabout." They walked all afternoon, coming to the Esplanade beside the leisurely, looping Swan River at sunset. Said thoughtful Jack Curtin: "Vance, you should have said where past history is written. This is where history is going to be written. Why don't you stay and help write it? Australia's big, Vance, not England. There's room to breathe here, to grow, to live."

Straight biography is also part of the profile:

> Jack Curtin was an Aussie who had to do things—and to have a cause for doing them. His cause was Socialism.
>
> He started out in staid and proper Melbourne—in the Melbourne Club, smoking in the dining room is still prohibited—but he started as a lowly printer's devil. In no time at all he was holding office in a union. Soon he was haunting Socialist Hall (smoking permitted) in Exhibition Street, watching the great orators sway their audiences, learning their tricks. . . .

And here is a close-up portrait:

> In the Prime Minister's office, a cool room with blue leather and a blue rug, a couple of etchings and a map, Jack Curtin affects a huge uncluttered desk. A reserved man, shunning formal gatherings, he nevertheless likes to cock one foot on the desk and talk at length. H

smokes incessantly—through a bamboo holder—and drinks tea without pause . . .

Time's human-interest devices are, of course, not all there are. Argument, for instance, lends itself very well to the discussion form—invented two thousand years ago by Plato. Scientific research is often made exciting as a sort of indoors adventure story. Educational material is best written by directly addressing the reader. (A handy example is the book you are reading now.) And there are many other ways of bringing in people.

But all these tricks do not help much if you want to make a given piece of impersonal prose humanly interesting without doing a complete rewrite job. What then? Is there any easy way out?

The thing to do in such a situation is to go through the text sentence by sentence and to look for the logical—not the grammatical—subject. After a while you will discover that the logical subject is always a person and that every sentence can be written so that this person is mentioned. Let's try this with another item from the same issue of *Time* which has, on the surface, almost no human interest:

> Du Pont this week announced a new product as highly potential as its nylon. It is wood impregnated with chemicals which transform it into a hard, polished material. Engineers call it "compreg."
>
> The treatment makes pine as hard as oak, oak as hard as ebony. Wood so treated does not warp, split, swell or shrink appreciably. It resists fire, rotting and termites, can be made as strong as many metals. It can be dyed any color so that it never needs painting or refinishing. If the surface is scratched, its glossy finish can be restored by sandpapering and buffing. Impregnated wood makes possible among other things, doors, windows, and drawers that do not stick or get loose.

Look at these sentences one by one. "Du Pont this week announced a new product as highly potential as its nylon."

Du Pont? The corporation? Certainly not: the announcing was done by Mr. So-and-so, their public relations man. How about "The Du Pont *people* announced . . ."?

Next: "It is wood impregnated with chemicals which transform it into a hard, polished material." Who impregnated the wood? The Du Pont people. Therefore: "*They* have impregnated wood with chemicals . . ." "Engineers call it 'compreg.'" That is: "*Their* engineers call it 'compreg.'"

"The treatment makes pine as hard as oak, oak as hard as ebony." Treatment by whom? Why not "With this treatment they can make pine as hard as oak, oak as hard as ebony"?

"Wood so treated does not warp, split, swell or shrink appreciably." To find the logical subject in such a sentence, you have to ask, How do you know? Well, how does anyone know a scientific fact? By testing. Every such statement can be reduced to a test somebody made at some time. (This is what philosophers call operationism.) So let's rewrite: "Their tests show that wood so treated does not warp," etc.

"It resists fire, rotting and termites, can be made as strong as many metals." The first half of this sentence refers again to tests; and the passive "can be made" translates easily into "*They* can make it . . ." Next: "It can be dyed any color so that it never needs painting or refinishing." Who would have to do the painting and refinishing? This is where the reader comes in: ". . . so that *you* never need to paint or refinish it." And again: 'If the surface is scratched, its glossy finish can be restored by sandpapering and buffing." This refers to anyone who is interested in the practical use of "compreg," and certainly also to the reader. Therefore: "If *you* scratch the surface, *you* can restore its glossy finish . . ."

And now the last sentence: "Impregnated wood makes possible among other things, doors, windows and drawers that do not stick or get loose." Possible for whom? For the public, the reader, you. "Among other things, impregnated wood will make it possible for *you* to have doors, windows, and drawers that do not stick or get loose."

Here is the whole passage with all personal references in their proper places:

> The Du Pont people announced this week a new product as highly potential as their nylon. They have impregnated wood with chemicals and transformed it into a hard, polished material. Their engineers call it "compreg."
>
> With this treatment, they can make pine as hard as oak, oak as hard as ebony. Their tests show that wood so treated does not warp, split, swell or shrink appreciably; it resists fire, rotting and termites. They can make it as strong as many metals and dye it any color so that you never need to paint or refinish it. If you scratch the surface, you can restore its glossy finish by sandpapering and buffing. Among other things, impregnated wood will make it possible for you to have doors, windows, and drawers that do not stick or get loose.

Naturally, this version is not as readable as if the story of "compreg" had been told by a dramatic description of its discovery; but even the few *theirs* and *yous* serve to point up the human interest that was buried in the original story.

The difference, as you see, is linguistic; and it can be measured by simply counting the proportion of *theirs* and *yous* and other references to people in the text. A practical method to do this is the following:

First, count all names of people. If the name consists of several words, count it as one, e.g., "Vice Admiral Frederick J. Horne." Next, count all personal pronouns except those that refer to things and not to people. Then count the human-interest words on this list:

> Man, woman, child; boy, girl, baby; gentleman, lady; sir, mister, madam(e), miss; guy, dame, lad, lass, kid.
>
> Father, mother, son, daughter, brother, sister, husband, wife, uncle, aunt, cousin, nephew, niece; family; parent; sweetheart; dad, daddy, papa, mamma.
>
> People (not peoples), folks, fellow, friend.

Count also combinations of these words with each other and with grand-, great grand-, step- and -in-law, and familiar forms of them like *grandpa*.

When you have found the number of these names, pronouns and human-interest words per 100 words of your text, you can check the degree of human interest against this table:

NUMBER OF PERSONAL REFERENCES PER 100 WORDS	
VERY EASY	19 or more
EASY	14
FAIRLY EASY	10
STANDARD	6
FAIRLY DIFFICULT	4
DIFFICULT	3
VERY DIFFICULT	2 or less

The standard of 6 personal references per 100 words is found, for instance, in feature articles in popular magazines. Very easy prose, for instance love stories in pulp magazines, runs to about 20 such words in 100: that means, every fifth word in such fiction refers to a person. Very difficult scientific material, of course, may be written without mentioning any persons at all. This book has 6 personal references in 100 words.

EXERCISE

Rewrite the rest of the article on impregnated wood to the human-interest standard of *Time* (about 8 personal references per 100 words):

> The product developed from research begun by the U. S. Forest Products Laboratory. The impregnating material, called methylolurea, is made principally from two cheap, plentiful chemicals—urea and formaldehyde—which are synthesized from coal, air and water. In the impregnating process, wood is pressed and soaked in methylolurea solution, which is converted by the wood's acids into hard, insoluble resins. The wood becomes brittle, but this disadvantage can be partly offset by impregnating only the outer part of the wood, leaving a resilient core.
>
> Impregnated wood is so cheap and versatile that Du

Pont claims it will compete with the much more expensive plastics and light metals. Moreover, the process will make usable vast resources of little-used soft woods—maples, poplars, gums, etc. The impregnation process simplifies the making of veneers and plywoods, because pressed and impregnated layers of wood need no glue.

Chapter VII

HERE'S YOUR YARDSTICK

WE HAVE talked about the three things that make for simple language—short sentences, few affixes, and many personal references—and this chapter, as you can easily guess, will tell you how to combine them into a yardstick. I hope you won't be terrified when you see that there is some figuring to be done; most of the mathematics have been worked out for you in the tables in the back of this book, so that all you have to do is some simple adding and subtracting. After a while, you will get the hang of the yardstick formula and will be able to guess the exact degree of difficulty of what you are reading or writing.

Here is how you figure a difficulty score: First, take the average length of the sentences and multiply it by .1338 (you can look this up on page 202). Then, take the number of affixes per 100 words and multiply it by .0645 (for this you use page 203). Add these two figures. Next, multiply the number of personal references in 100 words by .0659 (worked out on page 204) and subtract the result from the sum of the first two figures. Finally, subtract .75. The result is your difficulty score, which is apt to be a figure between 0 and 7. Here is what it means:

DIFFICULTY SCORE	
VERY EASY	up to 1
EASY	1 to 2
FAIRLY EASY	2 to 3
STANDARD	3 to 4
FAIRLY DIFFICULT	4 to 5
DIFFICULT	5 to 6
VERY DIFFICULT	6 or more

Now let's try an example. Let's start out with testing a rather difficult piece of writing; then let's shorten the sentences, reduce the affixes, and increase the number of references to people. Then when we are all through, let's test the passage again and see what we have accomplished.

Since you will have to reread this example five times, I chose a piece of writing that is an important historical document and of great interest to all of us: the famous Article VII of the Lend-Lease Agreement the United States made with Great Britain and most of the other United Nations. This article is the cornerstone of postwar international trade and certainly worth studying closely. Here is the original text. (To make our job easier, sentences are separated by /, affixes are hyphenated and printed in italics, and personal references are printed in capitals.)

> In the fin*al* *de*-term-*in*-*ation* of the *bene*-fits to be *pro*-vide-*d* to the Un-*ite*-*d* States of America by the Govern-*ment* of the Un-*ite*-*d* King-*dom* in *re*-turn for aid furn-*ish*-*ed* under the Act of *Con*-gress of March 11, 1941, the terms and *con*-di-*tions* there-*of* shall be such as not to burden *com*-merce *be*-tween the two countr-*ies*, but to *pro*-mote mutu-*al*-*ly* *ad*-vant-*age*-*ous* eco-*nom*-*ic* *re*-la-*tions* *be*-tween them and the bet-*ter*-*ment* of world-wide eco-*nom*-*ic* *re*-la-*tions*./ To that end, they shall *in*-clude *pro*-vis-*ion* for *a*-gree-*d* act-*ion* by the Un-*ite*-*d* States of America and the Un-*ite*-*d* King-*dom*, open to parti-*cip*-*ation* by all other countr-*ies* of like mind, *di*-rect-*ed* to the *ex*-pans-*ion*, by *ap*-propri-*ate* *inter*-nat-*ion*-*al* and dom-*estic* meas-*ures*, of *pro*-duct-*ion*, *em*-ploy-*ment*, and the *ex*-change and *con*-sump-*tion* of goods, which are the mater-*ial* found-*ations* of the liber-*ty* and welfare of all peoples; to the *e*-limin-*ation* of all forms of *dis*-crimin-*at*-*ory* treat-*ment* in *inter*-nat-*ion*-*al* *com*-merce, and to the *re*-duct-*ion* of tariffs and other trade barr-*iers*; and, in gener-*al*, to the *at*-tain-*ment* of all the eco-*nom*-*ic* *ob*-ject-*ives* set for-*th* in the Join-*t* *De*-clar-*ation* made on August 12, 1941, by the *Pre*-sid-*ent* of the Un-*ite*-*d*

States of America and the Prime Min-*ister* of the Un-*ite-*
King-*dom.*/

At an ear-*ly* *con*-ven-*ient* date, *con*-vers-*ations* shall b
be-gun *be*-tween the two Govern-*ments* with a view to *de*
term-*in-ing*, in the light of govern-*ing* eco-*nom-ic* *con*-di
tions, the be-*st* means of *at*-tain-*ing* the *a*-bove-state-
ob-ject-*ives* by their own *a*-gree-*d* act-*ion* and of seek-*in*
the *a*-gree-*d* act-*ion* of other like-mind-*ed* govern-*ments.*

Now let's test the difficulty of this text. It has 242 word
3 sentences, 139 affixes, and not a single reference to a perso
as such (it speaks of the President and the Prime Ministe
but not of Mr. Roosevelt and Mr. Churchill). In other word
the average length of a sentence is 81 words, there are 5
affixes in every 100 words, and no personal references at al
For sentences of 81 words, we find (on page 202) the figur
10.84; for 57 affixes (on page 203), 3.68, which adds up to 14.5
Now we subtract from this 0 for personal references (there ar
none) and .75 (the constant), which makes 13.77, our difficult
score for this passage. As you see, this is way beyond 6, th
lowest score for VERY DIFFICULT writings. In other words, th
thing is completely unreadable diplomatic double talk. It
worth simplifying all right.

To start our simplification, we first break up the sentence
leaving everything else untouched. Now it reads like this:

> The benefits to be provided to the United States
> America by the Government of the United Kingdom
> return for aid furnished under the Act of Congress
> March 11, 1941, will be finally determined./
>
> The terms and conditions of these benefits shall
> such as not to burden commerce between the two cou
> tries, but to promote mutually advantageous econom
> relations between them and the betterment of worl
> wide economic relations./
>
> To that end, these terms and conditions shall inclu
> provisions for agreed action by the United States and t
> United Kingdom, open to participation by all oth
> countries of like mind./

> This action shall be directed to the expansion, by appropriate international and domestic measures, of production, employment, and the exchange and production of goods (which are the material foundations of the liberty and welfare of all peoples)./
>
> It shall also be directed to the elimination of all forms of discriminatory treatment in international commerce, and to the reduction of tariffs and other trade barriers./
>
> And, in general, it shall be directed to the attainment of all the economic objectives set forth in the Joint Declaration made on August 12, 1941, by the President of the United States of America and the Prime Minister of the United Kingdom./
>
> At an early convenient date, conversations shall be begun by the two governments./
>
> These conversations shall be held with a view to determining, in the light of governing economic conditions, the best means of attaining the above-stated objectives by their own agreed action and of seeking the agreed action of other like-minded governments./

To get our sentences shorter, we had to repeat certain words, so that we now have 259 words and 8 sentences, or 32 words to a sentence. These sentences are still too long and difficult to read, as we see from the table on page 38. However, once we get going with our next step (throwing out affixes) we shall also cut down on unnecessary words and circumlocutions so that our sentences will become shorter in the process.

Now let us translate this version by using root words instead of affix words wherever we can. Let's keep a few key words, like "economic" and be ruthless against all others:

> What America gets back from England for Lend-Lease aid will be sett-*le-d* in the end.
>
> This shall be done in such a way that trade *be*-tween the two countr-*ies* gets eas-*i-er*, and eco-*nom-ic* ties that are good for them and the whole world, get strong-*er*.
>
> America and England shall work out a plan for that in which other countr-*ies* of like mind may take part.

> They shall plan to take steps, by themselves and *to*-gether, for more goods and jobs and more trade and use of goods.
>
> *Al*-so, they shall plan to do *a*-way with all ways of treat-*ing* the trade of some countr-*ies* bett-*er* than that of others, and to make tariffs and other trade barr-*iers* low-*er*.
>
> And anyway, they shall plan for the eco-*nom-ic* aims of the Atlant-*ic* Chart-*er*.
>
> As soon as it can be done, the two govern-*ments* shall start talk-*ing*.
>
> They shall look at the eco-*nom-ic* facts as they will be then; and they shall try to find the be-*st* means of mak-*ing* all these things come *a*-bout by their own plan and of mak-*ing* other like-mind-*ed* govern-*ments* plan with them.

This version, of course, is where most of our simplification has been done. This is only natural, since it is affixes that make diplomatic language so highfalutin and abstract—and that make it possible to use a lot of words without saying anything much. In figures, here is what happened: We used now 185 words and 32 affixes, or 17 affixes in 100 words. And prose with 17 affixes per 100 words, as the table on page 43 shows, is more than VERY EASY; in fact, it is the easiest kind of English you are apt to come across anywhere.

And now let's go one step further and put references to people in all the proper places. In an international treaty, that's very easy; we simply remember what a treaty is: something put on paper by the spokesmen of two nations. Therefore, it is only correct that we put *we* and *us* in place of *their* and *them* and make this agreement a personal affair. After all, it isn't the countries that agree—the mountains, rivers, and plains—but the people of these countries. So let us rewrite:

> In the end, WE will settle what America gets back from England for Lend-Lease aid.
>
> WE shall do this in such a way that trade between OUR

> two countries gets easier, and economic ties that are good for US and the whole world, get stronger.
>
> WE shall work out a plan for that in which other countries of like mind may take part.
>
> WE shall plan to take steps, by OURSELVES and together, for more goods and jobs and more trade and use of goods.
>
> Also, WE shall plan to do away with all ways of treating the trade of some countries better than that of others, and to make tariffs and other trade barriers lower.
>
> And anyway, WE shall plan for the economic aims of the Atlantic Charter.
>
> As soon as it can be done, spokesmen of OUR two governments shall start talking.
>
> THEY shall look at the economic facts as they will be then; and THEY shall try to find the best means of making all these things come about by THEIR own plan and of making other like-minded governments plan with THEM.

Now, instead of no references to people, people are mentioned 14 times within 185 words, or 8 times per 100 words. Let's look at the table on page 56 to see what this means: we have now made our text FAIRLY EASY as far as human interest goes.

To finish up the job, let us rearrange this version into a more logical pattern, and add a few conversational touches. Then we get:

> As soon as it can be done, WE will start talk*ing* *a*bout how England shall pay America for Lend-Lease aid./ WE shall look at the eco-*nom-ic* facts as they will be then;/ and WE shall try to work out a plan for OUR own countr*ies* and others who want to go *a*long, to do these things:/
>
> WE shall plan, *with*-in each countr-*y* and *be*-tween countr-*ies*, for more jobs and for mak-*ing*, trad-*ing* and us-*ing* more goods./ *Al*-so, WE shall plan to do *a*-way with

all ways of treat-*ing* the trade of some countr-*ies* bett-*er* than that of others, and to low-*er* tariffs and other trade barr-*iers*./

This way WE shall ease trade *be*-tween OUR two countr-*ies*, streng-*th-en* eco-*nom*-ic ties that will help US and the whole world and, in gener-*al*, work to-*ward* the eco-*nom-ic* aims of the Atlant-*ic* Chart-*er*./

Now we have 139 words, 6 sentences, 32 affixes and 9 personal references. This gives an average sentence of 23 words, 23 affixes per 100 words, and 6 personal references per 100 words. To find the final difficulty score, we figure like this:

	3.08	(from table on page 202)
plus	1.48	(from table on page 203)
	4.56	
minus	.40	(from table on page 204)
minus	.75	(constant)
	3.41	

The score of 3.41 means that we have managed to simplify that unreadable diplomatic doubletalk to STANDARD, well readable English. It takes a little time to recognize the original in our final version, but that difference has its advantages: the translation shows up a few things that were well hidden between high-sounding words. For instance: the agreement does *not* include a plan for repayment of Lend-Lease aid; it leaves the making of such a plan to another conference or conferences some time in the future; and, most important, it says that payment will depend on what the world will *then* look like economically. If you didn't get all that when you first read the original version of Article VII, then plain talk has already paid you a little dividend in your understanding of current events. And maybe you will not be disappointed because this chapter turned out to be all work and no fun.

And now, if you want to do some

Exercise

Use the directions for using the yardstick formula that are summarized on pages 195 to 205, and test the three intermediate versions in this chapter to see how they compare with the original and the final version. Or, if you prefer, apply the yardstick to other excerpts in this book or samples from your own writing or reading. Incidentally, the score for this book is 3.39.

P.S. For Those Who Hate Figures

If you want a quick rule-of-thumb yardstick without much figuring, here is what you do:

Take the average number of affixes per 100 words, subtract the average number of personal references in 100 words, and divide by two. Then add the average number of words per sentence. Check the result against this scale:

Very Easy	up to 13
Easy	13 to 20
Fairly Easy	20 to 29
Standard	29 to 36
Fairly Difficult	36 to 43
Difficult	43 to 52
Very Difficult	52 or more

Chapter VIII

LIVE WORDS

YOU now know the recipe for simplicity: Talk about people in short sentences with many root words. Here is an easy trick for killing these three birds with one stone: Use verbs. Let me repeat that: *Use verbs.*

Nothing is as simple as a brief three-word sentence that follows the pattern: somebody *does* something. It is the verb that gives life to any sentence; it literally makes the sentence go.

But we have seen that in Chinese, the simplest of all languages, there is no such thing as a verb (or noun or adjective, for that matter). How, then, do the Chinese make their sentences go? Well, the explanation is simple: one word in each sentence serves, so to speak, as its motor; for this particular sentence, it works as a verb. If a Chinese says "Man bite dog," the word *bite*, otherwise unclassified, serves as a verb; that's why it has been put after *man* and before *dog*.

In modern English, which gets more and more "Chinese," we do that all the time and "appoint" a word to do verb service by putting it in a certain place in a sentence. We can say *Raise your face* or *Face your raise*; *Ship a book* or *Book a ship*; *Spot the cover* or *Cover the spot*. There is no question that each of these sentences has a verb in it, and no question which is the verb.

The point of all this is, of course, that I am talking here only of those words that are used as verbs in a sentence. They are what the grammarians call the "finite active verb forms" and they are the only ones that have life in them. Hearing of verbs, you probably think of passive participles and infinitives and gerunds and all the other fancy varieties that have plagued your grammar-school days. Well, forget about them: for all practical purposes they are not verbs, but nouns or adjectives—lifeless words that won't make your sentences move. The verbs you want to use are those that are in active business doing verb work; if you use a verb in the passive voice or make a participle or noun out of it, you have lost the most valuable part in the process: it's like cooking vegetables and throwing away the water with all the vitamins in it.

If you go through any newspaper or magazine and look for active, kicking verbs in the sentences, you will realize that this lack of well used verbs is the main trouble with modern English writing. Almost all nonfiction nowadays is written in a sort of pale, colorless sauce of passives and infinitives, motionless and flat as paper. Listen to this, for instance (from an essay by Paul Schrecker in the *Saturday Review of Literature*):

> Maybe the gradual actualization of this solidarity was the result of scientific and hence technological progress which caused distances to shrink and required ever-expanding markets. But it is a preconceived and entirely unwarranted idea to believe this technological unification to have been a primary cause, and hence to overlook the fact that its triumphant appearance on the world scene would not have been possible without the prior existence of a potential world-civilization. The ever-expanding sphere of influence of literature, science, and works of art, which rarely respects any national or regional boundaries, cannot be accounted for by the introduction of faster and easier means of communication or by the improved technological methods of mass reproduction. The phenomenon reveals mankind's preparedness to respond promptly to incentives emerging from the fields of knowledge and the arts, irrespective of their national and regional origin.

Or how about this (from "Mary Haworth's Mail"):

> Morbid preoccupation with thoughts of sex gratification, after one has attained the age of reason, is not a

> sign of emotional precocity, as some may suppose; but just the opposite, namely: evidence of a definitely infantile type of emotional egocentricity; what the psychologists call a state of arrested development. The uncomprehending inarticulate infant's sense of well being is wholly related to bodily feelings,—of being well fed, comfortably clothed and bedded, fondly caressed, etc. His sole concern, insistently registered, is with physical gratification, because instinct tells him that pleasurable sensations, at his helpless level of development, are synonymous with a reassuring sufficiency of creature care and healthy survival.

Now, if you look closely, you will notice that the only active, finite verbs in the first passage are *caused, required, respects,* and *reveals*: four mildly active verbs matched by 27 passive forms, infinitives, participles, verbs made into nouns, and forms of the auxiliary verb *to be.* In the second passage, we have *suppose, call,* and *tells,* against 32 inactive verb forms of various types.

And now let us look at the language of Shakespeare or the Bible, for contrast. Here is a speech by Brutus:

> No, not an oath; if not the face of men,
> The sufferance of our souls, the time's abuse,—
> If these be motives weak, break off betimes,
> And every man hence to his idle bed;
> So let high-sighted tyranny range on,
> Till each man drop by lottery. But if these,
> As I am sure they do, bear fire enough
> To kindle cowards, and to steel with valour
> The melting spirits of women, then, countrymen,
> What need we any spur, but our own cause
> To prick us to redress? what other bond,
> Than secret Romans, that have spoke the word,
> And will not palter? and what other oath,
> Than honesty to honesty engag'd,
> That this shall be, or we will fall for it?
> Swear priests, and cowards, and men cautelous,

Old feeble carrions and such suffering souls
That welcome wrongs; unto bad causes swear
Such creatures as men doubt; but do not stain
The even virtue of our enterprise,
Nor the insuppressive mettle of our spirits,
To think that or our cause or our performance
Did need an oath; when every drop of blood
That every Roman bears, and nobly bears,
Is guilty of a several bastardy,
If he do break the smallest particle
Of any promise that hath pass'd from him.

And these are words of Job:

Wherefore do the wicked live, become old, yea, are mighty in power?

Their seed is established in their sight with them, and their offspring before their eyes.

Their houses are safe from fear, neither is the rod of God upon them.

Their bull gendereth, and faileth not; their cow calveth, and casteth not her calf.

They send forth their little ones like a flock, and their children dance.

They take the timbrel and harp, and rejoice at the sound of the organ.

They spend their days in wealth, and in a moment go down to the grave.

Therefore they say unto God, Depart from us; for we desire not the knowledge of thy ways.

What is the Almighty, that we should serve him? and what profit should we have, if we pray unto him?

Lo, their good is not in their hand: the counsel of the wicked is far from me.

How oft is the candle of the wicked put out! and how oft cometh their destruction upon them! God distributeth sorrows in his anger.

They are as stubble before the wind, and as chaff that the storm carrieth away.

Clearly, most of the power, movement, and beauty of these passages comes from the succession of active verbs: Shakespeare makes tyranny *range*, men *drop*, and a cause *prick us to redress*; the Bible makes a bull *gender*, a cow *calve*, and children *dance*. There are 19 live verbs in the Shakespeare passage against 11 passive verb forms, verbal nouns, etc.; in the Bible passage the ratio is 20 to 11.

Maybe you will say that I am unfair in using the Bible and Shakespeare as examples. After all, newspapers and magazine articles are written to meet a deadline, by writers who don't dream of being literary geniuses; so why compare their style with all-time masterpieces? I admit I am a little biased here; but anybody can try to use active, working verbs wherever possible. It won't make him a Shakespeare but it will make him write good, plain English. Here is, for instance, one modern example from Ernie Pyle:

> The company I was with got its orders to rest about 5 one afternoon. They dug foxholes along the hedgerows, or commandeered German ones already dug. Regardless of how tired you may be, you always dig in the first thing.
>
> Then they sent some men with cans looking for water. They got more K rations up by jeep, and sat on the ground eating them.
>
> They hoped they would stay there all night, but they weren't counting on it too much. Shortly after supper a lieutenant came out of a farmhouse and told the sergeants to pass the word to be ready to move in 10 minutes. They bundled on their packs and started just before dark.
>
> Within half an hour they had run into a new fight that lasted all night. They had had less than four hours' rest in three solid days of fighting. That's the way life is in the infantry.

There are 16 working verbs there and not a single verb form or noun that could, or should, be turned into an active finite verb. And now compare it with this sentence from a popular article on economics:

In somewhat over-simplified technical terms, inflation is caused by the existence, at any given time in an economic system, of an aggregate of *effective* purchasing power greater than the aggregate of the goods and services for sale.

What a definition! "Inflation" is caused by the *existence* of an *aggregate* that is *greater* than another *aggregate*. This hows clearly how impossible it is to describe a process—omething happening—without using a single active verb. Obviously the writer realized that himself, because the next entence reads like this:

> . . . When we add up the amounts of cash and credit of all kinds at the disposal of everybody who is ready to buy something, and find that the sum is larger than the sum of all the things to be bought at existing prices, then prices are likely to go up.

Now the verbs are in their proper places, and everything ecomes crystal-clear: First we *add* something, then we *fird* hat it is larger than something else, and then prices will *go p*. This is the classic type of scientific explanation: If you do X and Y, what happens is Z. (Or, in the De Kruif manner: The great scientist did X and Y, and what happened was Z.)

And now, let's get down to work and try to rewrite a verbless" passage ourselves. Here is another bit from the terary essay I quoted on page 67:

> Integrated into the circulation of national life much more completely than any other modern literature, American belles-lettres also give a much more faithful and adequate picture of the entire civilization to which they belong than literature abroad, whose very compliance with—or willful opposition to—traditions that have long lost their anchorage in the depths of their respective national civilizations, renders them unable to keep abreast of the rejuvenated spirit of their epoch.

Here is the same sentence with the nouns made into verbs:

American belles-lettres circulate in the national life much more than other modern literatures do; they picture the entire civilization to which they belong more faithfully and adequately. The spirit of the times has become young again, and literatures abroad cannot keep abreast with it because of certain traditions they comply with or wilfully oppose. These traditions were once anchored in the depths of their national civilizations, but have lost that anchorage long ago.

And now I expect you to go ahead and pepper your speech and writing with active verbs. But before you start using this rule of thumb, let me warn you. There is one place where it does not work: in written dialogue. You know the sort of thing I mean:

"She is, I think, a lady not known to Monsieur," murmured the valet . . .

"Show her out here, Hippolyte," the Comte commanded . . .

"My descent upon you is unceremonious," she began . .

"But seat yourself, I beg of you, Mademoiselle," cried the Comte . . .

"But yes," she insisted . . .

"Certainly people are wrong," agreed the Comte . . .

"Perhaps," he murmured . . .

"The jewels!" she breathed . . .

Fowler, in his *Dictionary of Modern English Usage*, says that this mannerism was started by George Meredith; wher- ever it comes from, it is nowadays an excellent means to tel a bad novel from a good one. Apparently all bad writers d it and all good writers don't. Look at the fearless way in whic John Hersey repeats the word *said* in *A Bell for Adano*:

Zito said: "What is this Liberty Bell?"

Major Joppolo said: "It is the bell the Americans ran when they declared themselves free from the English."

Zito said: "The idea is good. But would America b willing to part with this bell for Adano?"

Major Joppolo said: "We would have to get a replica, Zito."

Zito said: "Describe this bell."

Major Joppolo said: "Well, it hangs in a tower in Philadelphia, I think . . ."

Imagine this with *Zito ventured* and *Major Joppolo reminisced* . . .

And now for your

EXERCISE

Translate the two passages on page 67 into plain English by making as many words as possible into active working verbs. Or try your hand at this second quote from "Mary Haworth's Mail":

> As nearly as I can make out, this is a case of deferred adolescence. Mentally you are abreast of your years or maybe a bit beyond. But emotionally or psychologically, you are still the fledgling 14 which you assiduously exemplify in your chosen garb. The conundrum is whether your unseasonable green-gourd personality is directly related to organic or glandular subnormality,—which is staying your physical development more or less at child level,—or whether it is, rather, the outpicturing of subconscious stubborn reluctance to grow up and thus take lasting leave of the special prerogatives and adulation you may have enjoyed as a charming child prodigy.

Chapter IX

CROWDED WORDS

VOLTAIRE once said: "The adjective is the enemy of the noun." This sentence is one of the most famous epigrams about language; many young journalists have been started off with it and taught to hunt adjectives in their copy.

It's a good rule, but a little confusing. The fact is, grammarians still can't agree on what an adjective is. If you say, for instance, *A ravishing math teacher,* some of them will tell you that *ravishing* and *math* are adjectives; some will say that *ravishing* is a verb form; some others will insist that *math* is a noun (if they admit it is a word at all). The best thing for us is to leave grammatical labels behind and see what the words do in and to a sentence. Then, at once, we see that *math* defines *teacher,* and that *ravishing* is a comment on the math teacher. In other words, there are two kinds of so-called adjectives: commenting and defining. Now we can see what Voltaire meant: obviously he didn't mean that a defining adjective is the enemy of the noun, because it really belongs to the noun (*What is she teaching?—Math*); in fact it is a part of the noun and you could just as well write *math-teacher,* with a hyphen. On the other hand, the commenting adjective is hostile to and literally kills the following noun: what we remember is that she is ravishing, not that she teaches math. If we want to "save" the noun from the commenting adjective, we have to write this description in two sentences: *She is ravishing. She is teaching math.*

As you see, the trouble with comment—whether adjective adverb, or anything else—is that it raises havoc with a sentence where it doesn't belong. In really simple language all sentences are just subject-predicate sentences: *Man bite dog. Man short. Dog tall.* If you make one sentence out of three and stick two comments into the first simple sentence (*Short man bite tall dog*), you are already on your way toward difficulty and sophistication. You force the reader, or listener, to take in three ideas in one sentence and you make understanding just so much harder. (James Joyce went even further and packed several ideas into one word, like *brooder-in-low* or *I was just thinkling upon that.*)

So our rule for plain talk is: Don't try to save a sentence by sticking a comment into another. Reason: two short sentences are easier to understand than one long one, with extra stuff in it.

I said in the beginning that newspapermen are now being taught that adjectives are Bad. The trouble is, they are also being taught to save words and so, after a while, they forget all about adjective hunting and become sentence stuffers. Here is a mild case:

> Married, he lives with his wife and three sons in New Jersey.

What he means is: *He is married and . . .*

Sometimes the two ideas don't match:

> The 53-year-old commentator left high school to carry copy on the Brooklyn Times.

Or:

> Kyser, bespectacled, was born thirty-eight years ago in Rocky Mountain, N.C.

Some writers habitually fill their sentences up to the brim. Here is an extract from a book review by Harrison Smith in the *Saturday Review of Literature* (I have put all the comments in italics):

> The two sisters, *island aristocrats, whose lifelong fate was sealed when they saw one morning in Saint Pierre a handsome boy of thirteen, whose father, an untidy but*

a heart-of-gold physician, had just returned a widower to his native town. Marguerite, *the younger of the sisters, a happy, blue-eyed, blonde child,* wins his love; Marianne, *dark, passionate, self-willed, determinedly* molds his life until he leaves the island, *a lieutenant in the Royal British Navy, bound for the China coast.* The young ladies sit behind and wait *frigidly* for over ten years for word from him. William, in the meantime, had been lured by a *half-caste* girl in a Chinese port into losing his ship and one morning, *penniless, half-naked, and drugged,* finds himself aboard a *clipper* ship, *bound for New Zealand, an exile.*

Sorted out, this reads:

Marguerite and Marianne were sisters. They were island aristocrats. Marguerite was the younger; she was a happy, blue-eyed, blonde child. Marianne was dark, passionate and self-willed.

One morning, in Saint Pierre, they saw a handsome boy of thirteen. His name was William and he was the son of an untidy physician with a heart of gold. His father had just become a widower and returned to his native town.

That moment sealed the lifelong fate of the sisters: Marguerite won the boy's love, Marianne molded his life.

Then, one day, William left the island. He had joined the Royal British Navy and become a lieutenant. Now he was bound for the China coast . . . etc. etc.

Or let's have a look at our friend from the last chapter, Mary Haworth:

Is it *fine philosophic* restraint or is it *craven* expediency to *tacitly* assent, as you have done so far, to your wife's *outre* performance, when you are confident it is part of a pattern of infidelity? If it were in truth the *large* reaction of a *nobly magnanimous* mind, would it be ac companied on the other hand by the *primitive male-egoist* emotional attitude that the marriage is wrecked for you, if she is indulging in a *passing* fancy, as you believe?

Have you feared *subconsciously* to force and face a showdown lest the *resultant* dissection of the marital relationship and her *possible* counter-charges confront you with a *shrewd and merciless* delineation of yourself as one *pallidly* devoid of *salient traits* of *thorough* masculinity?

Nearly all the key ideas have been put into commenting adjectives and adverbs. Here is another, more sophisticated example (from a film review by James Agee in the *Nation*):

> Very belatedly I want to say that "The Watch on the Rhine" seemed much better on the screen than it did, *almost identically*, on the stage—*though I still wished Henry James might have written it*; and that *I join with anyone whose opinion of* Paul Lukas' performance is superlative. Also that *a simple-hearted* friendliness *generated between audience and screen* at "This Is the Army" made that film happy *to see even when it was otherwise boring*; *though* I am among an *apparent* minority which feels that Warner Brothers' *cuddly-reverential* treatment of President Roosevelt—in "Mission to Moscow," "This Is the Army," and *the forthcoming* "Princess O'Rourke"—is subject to charges *certainly* of indecent exposure and, *quite possibly*, of alienation of affection.

If you read this without the italicized words, you will see that it still makes sense; but the real point of the whole passage is expressed in those casually tucked-in adjectives like *simple-hearted* or *cuddly-reverential.* Mind you, I don't say that this is bad writing; but it isn't plain talk either, by a long shot.

But how about descriptions, you say: How can you describe anything—a city, a landscape—without using descriptive commenting adjectives? How can you get away from the pat tern of "the flowery summer meadows, the lush cow-pastures, the quiet lakes and the singing streams, the friendly accessible mountains"? Simple: put your description in verbs, in predicates, in defining adjectives; don't comment but describe what happens; report, don't analyze.

Here is a description of America (from a *New York Times* editorial):

> It is small things remembered, the little corners of the land, the houses, the people that each one loves. We love our country because there was a little tree on a hill, and grass thereon, and a sweet valley below; because the hurdy-gurdy man came along on a sunny morning in a city street; because a beach or a farm or a lane or a house that might not seem much to others was once, for each of us, made magic. It is voices that are remembered only, no longer heard. It is parents, friends, the lazy chat of street and store and office, and the ease of mind that makes life tranquil. . . .
>
> It is stories told. It is the Pilgrims dying in their first dreadful winter. It is the Minute Man standing his ground at Concord Bridge, and dying there. It is the army in rags, sick, freezing, starving at Valley Forge. It is the wagons and the men on foot going westward over Cumberland Gap, floating down the great rivers, rolling over the great plains. It is the settler hacking fiercely at the primeval forest on his new, his own lands. It is Thoreau at Walden Pond, Lincoln at Cooper Union, and Lee riding home from Appomattox. . . .

In short, if you want to give descriptive detail in plain language, describe what you see, even using adjectives if you must; but don't stuff your descriptions down the reader's throat, whether he wants them or not, by filling all the odd corners and empty spots in your sentences with little dabs of observation.

Which brings us, of course, to *Time* magazine. As you know the little descriptive adjectives—*beady-eyed, thin-lipped*—are the hallmark of *Time*; its editors say that they help the reader get a better picture of what's going on in the world. Well, let's have a look:

> Bevin v. Bevan
>
> Ernest Bevin, *the bull elephant* of British labor, last week sat *bulkily silent, beadily watchful,* in the back row at a caucus of Parliament's Laborite members. The proposal: to expel from the Party *his homonym—pink, grizzled Welshman* Aneurin Bevan. The crime: Laborite Bevan's revolt against Labor Minister Bevin in the House of Commons.
>
> At the *tense and troubled* meeting, Aneurin Bevan refused to recant. He argued that if he were bounced, 15 other Laborites who sided with him would also have to go. All over Britain, he warned, labor unions were rising against *tough, truculent* Ernie Bevin's Defense Regulation 1-AA (five years in prison for strike fomenters).
>
> As Aneurin Bevan talked, Ernie Bevin *restlessly* shifted *his weight, impatiently* flung his *farm-hardened* hands about *in gestures he had long used to brush aside opponents, soundlessly* worked his *pudgy* lips. . . .

This is the first part of a story about a British antistrike regulation. But, because of the *Time* formula, the reader is allowed only a quick glimpse at the topic in a brief parenthesis. What he really learns from this first third of the story is that Bevin and Bevan have similar names (this is made the heading) and that Bevin, in contrast to Bevan, is a heavy man (this he gets from four comments, with slight variations upon the theme, plus two photographs of Bevin and Bevan to show what they look like). What the trouble is about, or what the arguments are on each side, he cannot even guess at this point.

Now, psychologists have found that one of the main troubles in reading is the "overpotency" of certain words. Since we always read a few words at a time, those that are specially effective or colorful tend to blot out the others. The result is often that we get a wrong impression or, at least, read an emphasis into the text that isn't there. So it's quite obvious that *Time* readers are apt to learn a lot about the faces, figures, hands, lips and eyes of world leaders, but are liable to misread or skip what these people do.

So, for plain talk, here is a special rule about *Time*style adjectives: Don't use any. People will get you better without them.

And now, as your

Exercise

Rewrite, without commenting words, the rest of the passage on page 75 and the passages on pages 76 and 77.

Chapter X

EMPTY WORDS

THE Chinese, as we have seen, call the words that mean something "full words" and those that are just grammatical gadgets, "empty words." Naturally, each empty word adds a little grammar the reader or listener has to cope with; and each empty word saved saves time and effort at the receiving end.

Look closer at these empty words (the grammarians call them prepositions, conjunctions, adverbs, etc.). We use them all the time and much more than other words; that's why most people think that these words must be fully familiar to anyone who has any knowledge of English. Therefore, they think they must be the easiest words in the language.

Of course, it's just the other way around. When we read *elephant,* all we have to do is to think of a big animal with a trunk; but when we read *unless,* it means: see what is happening in the next clause; then think back to what happened in the main sentence; and then cancel that in your mind, but not quite.

So there is trouble enough with these empty words. But, odd as it may seem, plenty of writers go out of their way to use two or three of them instead of one wherever they can. This is what is known as "compound prepositions and conjunctions"; for instance, *in the case of* instead of *if,* or *for the purpose of* instead of *for.* Fowler, in his *Dictionary of Modern English Usage,* has this to say about them: "They are almost the worst element in modern English, stuffing up the newspaper columns with a compost of nouny abstractions. To young writers the discovery of these forms of speech, which are used very little in talk and very much in print, brings an expansive sense of increased power . . . Later, they know better, and realize that it is feebleness, instead of power, that they have been developing; but by that time the fatal ease that the compound-preposition style gives (to the writer, that is) has become too dear to be sacrificed."

So let's make a little list of what to avoid in plain talk:

along the lines of	instead of	*like*
as to	" "	*about*
for the purpose of	" "	*for*
for the reason that	" "	*since*
from the point of view of	" "	*for*
inasmuch as	" "	*since*
in favor of	" "	*for*
in order to	" "	*to*
in accordance with	" "	*by*
in the case of	" "	*if*
in the event that	" "	*if*
in the nature of	" "	*like*
in terms of	" "	*in*
on the basis of	" "	*by*
prior to	" "	*before*
with a view to	" "	*to*
with reference to	" "	*about*
with regard to	" "	*about*
with the result that	" "	*so that*

Of course, this is not a complete list; and sometimes we can replace the listed compounds by other words than those suggested or do without empty words altogether. But this may give you something to go by.

And here is a special reminder: Don't use a preposition before an indirect question if you can help it. Here are two examples from the same newspaper issue to show you what I mean:

> To my mind these concrete examples provide an objecjective *test of whether* Governor Dewey is fitted to take over the conduct of American policy in the climax and crisis of the war. (Walter Lippmann)
>
> The President also asked Pope many detailed questions about various sections behind the lines in Italy, especially

in regard to how the Italian population in those areas would receive American troops, and what cooperation they would give in rising up against the Nazis. (Drew Pearson)

And this is a nice bit of *of-which-of* from a government regulation:

> The determination *of which of* these regulations was applicable to the supply of a particular service depended upon the end use of the product upon which the service was rendered.

There is another group of empty words that are much discussed in the grammar and usage books: the so-called connectives, the little words that tie clauses and sentences together. English teachers will tell you that a handy stock of connectives is one of the best things for a good, clear style; as long as you stick to your *moreovers* and *indeeds*, you are all right.

But here again, if you go by the rules, your style will become more complex instead of simpler. In the first place, none of the books mention that there are really two sets of these connectives: one set that is used in everyday speech, and another set used almost exclusively in print. Here they are:

Plain talk:	*Bookish:*
and	*likewise*
besides, also	*in addition*
now, next	*moreover*
then	*furthermore*
but	*nevertheless*
however	*rather*
in other words	*that is to say*
for example	*more specifically*
in fact	*indeed*
of course	*to be sure*
so	*for this reason*
and so	*accordingly, consequently*
therefore	*hence, thus*

There are other connectives of both types, of course, bu
these are about all you will ever need for a simple styl
What's more, if you write simply, with the sentences properl
strung together, you will hardly need connectives. Englis
teachers will tell you that you can't do that because the reade
needs the connectives as guideposts; but never mind them. A
long as you use plain talk, no reader will know the differenc
For instance, do you miss any connectives in this piece fror
Samuel Grafton's column? It's closely reasoned all right, bu
he does it without "guideposts":

> What the subsidy-haters hate most about subsidies i
> their scientific nature. Subsidies, at least theoreticall
> apply the medicine only where it is needed and only i
> the amount needed. If bean-raisers need a bit more c
> money, the subsidy plan gives it to them, precisely, speci
> ically, and in measured quantity. The opposition prefe
> to help the bean-grower by raising all prices. It wants t
> assist the poor family in the side street by giving a $1
> bill to everybody in town.
>
> The difference is between a medicinal use of stimular
> and a general issue of grog to all hands. The subsidy pla
> would merely raise up those who are faint; the oppositio
> wants to have a party.
>
> The scientific, limited and factual nature of subsid
> operation is offensive to the kind of hunch-player wh
> draws his daily inspiration with his bath. What! Are w
> to study each case separately on its merits, and come to
> decision on the facts? Nothing could be more hateful t
> the wholesale type of thinker, who believes that a touc
> of inflation will solve all economic problems, while
> return to state government will solve all political ones.
>
> These characters have a credo of their own. It go
> something like this:
>
> 1. All college professors are quaint little monkeys, o
> of a fiction story by Clarence Budington Kelland. The
> invariably wear rubbers on sunny days, and forget the
> only when it rains.

2. The accumulated economic and political wisdom of the ages, as massed in books, cannot compare with the accumulated wisdom of the smoking car: Pullman, not Aristotle, is their inspiration.

3. "Research" is a comic word, and "statistics" is a laugh. Any study or report longer than a *Reader's Digest* article is, ipso facto, funny. The use by an official of an unfamiliar word indicates the inferiority, not of the reader, who does not understand it, but of the official, who does.

4. The business of statesmen is not to solve problems, but to win arguments.

The use of subsidies is peculiarly galling to men of these beliefs, because it involves the use of the scientific method. . . .

And now, just for the fun of it, let's put fancy connectives wherever we can:

What the subsidy-haters hate most about subsidies is their scientific nature. That is to say, subsidies, at least theoretically, apply the medicine only where it is needed and only in the amount needed. Thus, if bean-raisers need a bit more of money, the subsidy plan gives it to them, precisely, specifically, and in measured quantity. Nevertheless, the opposition prefers to help the bean-grower by raising all prices. More specifically, it wants to assist the poor family in the side street by giving a $10 bill to everybody in town.

That is to say, the difference is between a medicinal use of stimulant and a general issue of grog to all hands. More specifically, the subsidy plan would merely raise up those who are faint; whereas, the opposition wants to have a party.

Thus, the scientific, limited and factual nature of subsidy operations is offensive to the kind of hunch-player who draws his daily inspiration with his bath. What! he might say; are we to study each case separately on its merits, and come to a decision on the facts? To be sure,

> nothing could be more hateful to the wholesale type of thinker, who believes that a touch of inflation will solve all economic problems, while a return to state government will solve all political ones.
>
> Indeed, these characters have a credo of their own. It goes something like this:
>
> 1. In the first place, all college professors are quaint little monkeys, out of a fiction story by Clarence Budington Kelland. Consequently, they invariably wear rubbers on sunny days, and forget them only when it rains.
>
> 2. In the second place, the accumulated economic and political wisdom of the ages, as massed in books, cannot compare with the accumulated wisdom of the smoking car. That is to say, Pullman, not Aristotle, is their inspiration.
>
> 3. Moreover, "research" is a comic word and "statistics" is a laugh. More specifically, any study or report longer than a *Reader's Digest* article is, ipso facto, funny. Likewise, the use by an official of an unfamiliar word indicates the inferiority, not of the reader, who does not understand it, but of the official, who does.
>
> 4. Furthermore, the business of statesmen is not to solve problems, but to win arguments.
>
> Consequently, the use of subsidies is peculiarly galling to men of these beliefs, because it involves the use of the scientific method. . . .

I hope you agree that the whole thing is now spoiled by the connectives. Here is, for the sake of balance, another columnist, Westbrook Pegler, in a colloquial mood:

> The way it began, why this fellow was a kind of side hill farmer down where the Government has been improving people and when the war come he went into a cotton factory and got to be a real good operator and he was making top money for the kind of job he was doing. Then the Government come in and built a lot of model homes and they assigned him to a house at a rent of $18 a month because he was underprivileged.

So one day the War Labor Board came along and pretty soon the manager of this factory he got a long letter and a lot of figures like a life insurance policy, and he was ordered to raise wages five cents an hour up to so much, but he is so busy making cloth for the war he don't read it very close so this fellow who is getting improved, why his pay goes up $11.20 a month, too. Well, he and the old lady felt pretty good about this.

But then comes the first of the month and the rent goes up from $18 a month to $25 and they figured it was just a mistake because it is the law that rents are frozen and old Sam certainly wouldn't be the one to violate his own laws and set people a bad example. . . .

I could spoil this one too by putting in a lot of bookish connectives, but I think you see by now what I mean.

A third kind of empty words you should know about are relative pronouns. This is where the famous difference between *that* and *which* comes in. The principle is easy: *which* is the bookish pronoun and *that* is the plain one. Most people get shy of *that* when they write for publication, and most people forget about *which* when they talk. The reason is this: *which* starts a commenting clause, and in plain, everyday talk, as we have seen, we don't stuff our sentences with comments. So *which* has become the literary of the two words, and now writers use it everywhere, even where the relative clause doesn't comment and they would naturally say *that* in conversation. For instance, somebody might mention corporations that have to file certain blanks with the government, using *that* without the slightest doubt. But a government writer will say:

CORPORATIONS WHICH MUST MAKE RETURN ON FORM 1121.

And after that, he will use all the empty words he can possibly get in, in their most elaborate forms and fanciest variations:

Every corporation required by section 52 to make a return, having an excess profits net income (computed under the invested capital credit method) of *more than* $5,000, or *in the case of* a mutual insurance company (*other than* life or marine) *which* is an interinsurer or reciprocal underwriter, of *more than* $50,000, except the following corporations, *which* under *the provisions of* section 727, are exempt from excess profits tax, *unless such* corporations are members of an affiliated group of corporations filing consolidated returns under section 141. . . .

Here is the climax:

Section 736 (a) provides that *in the case of* any taxpayer computing income from installment sales under *the method provided by* section 44 (a), if *such* taxpayer establishes, *in accordance with* regulations *prescribed* by the Commissioner *with the approval of* the Secretary, that the average *volume of* credit extended to purchasers *on the* installment *plan* in the four taxable years *preceding* the first taxable year beginning after December 31, 1941 was *more than* 125 percent of *the volume of such* credit extended to *such* purchasers in the taxable year, or the average outstanding installment accounts receivable at the end of each of the four taxable years *preceding* the first taxable year *beginning* after December 31, 1941, was *more than* 125 percent of *the amount of such* accounts receivable at the end of the taxable year, or if the taxpayer was *not in existence* for four previous taxable years the taxable years *during which* the taxpayer was *in existence, in either case* including only such years for *which* the income was computed under *the method provided in* section 44 (a), it may elect, in its excess profits tax return for the taxable year, to compute, *in accordance with* regulations *prescribed* by the Commissioner *with the approval of* the Secretary, its income from installment sales *on the basis of* the taxable period for *which such* income is accrued, *in lieu of the basis provided by* section 44 (a).

am sure the writer of this sentence would feel downright nsulted if you asked him to change it to something like 'Section 736 (a) says that if any taxpayer computes his installment-sales income under section 44 (a). . . ." But he would ertainly consider it a sin if you asked him to write ". . . only he years the income was computed for. . . ." Preposition at he end of a sentence! he will cry, and he will think he got ou there.

But don't be afraid: Prepositions at the end of sentences ave been used by all great English writers for over six hunlred years. Shakespeare wrote:

Such bitter business as the day
Would quake to look on

The Bible (King James Version) has:

I will not leave thee, until I have done that which I have spoken to thee of.

ind so it goes. George Oliver Curme, a leading American rammarian, says: "For many centuries the position of a reposition at or near the end of a proposition has been one f the outstanding features of our language." Fowler, in his *)ictionary of Modern English Usage,* starts the article "Prepsition at End" like this: "It is a cherished superstition that repositions must, in spite of the incurable English instinct or putting them late . . . be kept true to their name and laced before the word they govern." And Logan Pearsall mith, the famous stylist, asks us to appreciate "how consonant vith our English speech-rhythms" the preposition at the end s, and "what vigour and conciseness it adds, when skilfully ised, to our phrasing."

In fact, it's the greatest advantage of *that* over *which* that ou can leave it out and make your sentences simpler and nore colloquial by putting prepositions at the end. Many ood writers use this trick effectively. Here are a few examples:

From *Time* magazine:

> Out of Moscow came an agreement of such scope a few men had dared hope for.

From a spy story by Manning Coles:

> There's been a little bit of funny business going o down here nobody seems to get to the bottom of.

From an article on co-operatives by Horace M. Kallen:

> Fundamentally, the members of the Toad Lane Societ had not liberated themselves from the ways of thinkin and feeling of the producer economy they had grown u in and were the victims of.

From a film review by David Lardner:

> A fact to be noted right here is that the movie i apparently giving its all-out support to astrology, a stan not everybody may be ready to go along with.

From Earl Wilson's column "It Happened Last Night":

> I tried to buy a copy [of *Strange Fruit*] in the Ol Corner Bookstore [in Boston].
>
> "I wouldn't sell it to you because you might be a polic officer," a salesman told me.
>
> This is the nicest thing I've ever been accused o posing as.

If you want a good test to find out whether you are usin too many empty words in your writing, here is a suggestion Imagine you are writing poetry instead of prose. A poet, yo see, needs strong, meaningful words; empty grammatical gadg ets just clutter up a poem and make it sound like prose How do you like, for instance, this piece of poetry:

> Nevertheless, in the last analysis
> You must bring Freedom in to your hearth in order tha
> it may burn
> To the same extent as a cut hickory log; likewise, yo
> must put on

Democracy in the same manner as a patched as well as
friendly coat;
In addition, you must bring Sacrifice down so as to reach
street-level
And, thereupon, sweep with it, in such a way as a cloud-
broom made usual;
Finally, you must pour Liberty warm into the bottle
At which your infant has suckled.

Yes, you guessed right: I stuffed it with empty words. This is the original (from *The Great and Marching Words* by Christopher La Farge):

Yet in the end
You must bring Freedom in to your hearth to burn
Like a cut hickory log, you must put on
Democracy like a patched and friendly coat,
You must bring Sacrifice down to street-level
And sweep with it, like a cloud-broom made usual,
You must pour Liberty warm into the bottle
Your infant's suckled at.

Exercise

Rewrite the sentence from the excess-profits tax instructions on page 88 using as few and as simple empty words as possible

Chapter XI

THE GLAMOUR OF PUNCTUATION

SOME time ago, Sylvia F. Porter, the financial reporter, wrote a *Reader's Digest* article on the income-tax nightmare. Among other things, she said, "there's an improvement upon which all agree. And that is exiling from Washington forever the writers of the incredible thing called income tax prose and making it mandatory for the new authors of tax instruction sheets to use (1) short words, (2) short sentences, (3) no semicolons and (4) no parentheses."

The first two of these points are fine, of course; but the last two just go to show that the average writer considers punctuation marks an invention of the devil that makes everything more complex and harder to understand.

That's an odd idea. After all, when people started writing, they just put one word after the other; as for punctuation, the reader was on his own. Only later writers marked their copy with little dots and dashes and started to give the reader a break. And now people complain that punctuation makes reading harder!

I think the reason must be that punctuation, to most people, is a set of arbitrary and rather silly rules you find in printers' style books and in the back pages of school grammars. Few people realize that it is the most important single device for making things easier to read.

When we are talking, of course, we don't use any punctuation marks. We use a system of shorter or longer pauses between words to join or separate our ideas, and we raise or lower our voices to make things sound emphatic or casual. In other words, we make ourselves understood not only by words but also by pauses and by stress or pitch.

Punctuation gets pauses and stress (but not pitch) down on paper. The system is simple to get the hang of:

<table>
<tr><th></th><th>Between Words</th><th>Between Sentences</th></tr>
<tr><td>Normal pause</td><td>White space</td><td>Period</td></tr>
<tr><td>Shorter pause</td><td>Hyphen</td><td>Semicolon (or colon)</td></tr>
<tr><td>Longer pause</td><td>Dash</td><td>Paragraph</td></tr>
<tr><td>Normal stress</td><td colspan="2">Normal type (or writing)</td></tr>
<tr><td>Unstressed</td><td colspan="2">Parentheses (or two dashes)</td></tr>
<tr><td>Stressed</td><td colspan="2">Italics (or underlining)</td></tr>
</table>

Let me explain this little table: As long as you use normal pauses and normal stress in talking, don't use anything but periods and commas in writing. When you run two or more words together with almost no pause between them (because you use them in that sentence as one word), hyphenate them. When you use a longer pause—Watch out for the next word! —make a dash. Same with sentences: When you run two or more sentences together (because you use a string of sentences as one), use a semicolon or, if the first sentence introduces the second, a colon. When you use a longer pause—Now comes something else!—make a paragraph. And don't forget to use italics or parentheses for emphasis or casual mention.

When you put plain talk in writing, two punctuation marks are particularly important for you: hyphens and semicolons. The reason is this: The fewer empty words you use and the more you rely on word order, the more important it is for you to show which words belong closely together; this you do by using hyphens. On the other hand, in plain talk you often use two or more short sentences instead of one long one and show the connection by semicolons.

Here is for instance a collection of hyphenated expressions from a colloquial piece on Wendell Willkie:

> . . . this now-you-see-it-now-you-don't impression . . . no Landon-like also-ran obscurity . . . the big-shaggy-bear manner . . . the verbal give-and-take of a lawyer . . . passion for face-to-face debate . . . the halcyon, high-wide-

> and-handsome days of Wall Street . . . a financial-district Democrat . . . a Willkie-packed audience . . . Steve Hannagan of bathing-beauty fame . . . tailoring his words to his on-the-spot listeners . . . it was a heads-I-win-tails-you-lose proposition . . . his forty-nine-day junket around the globe . . . slow, unglamorous, personal-contact stuff . . . a twentieth-century Henry Clay . . .

As you see, hyphens come in handy when you want just to hint at a general idea or quickly describe an impression. Here is a good example from Westbrook Pegler:

> . . . one of those continued-among-the-leather-belting-ads analyses in Fortune . . .

Another from a *Harper's* article on de Gaulle:

> Churchill apparently succeeded in explaining away the no-longer-a-great-power clause in the Smuts speech and at the same time persuading de Gaulle that it was to his interest to support the bloc-of-Western-Europe policy it announced.

And, of course, this just-to-give-you-the-idea device is a boon for reviewers. Here are two examples from David Lardner's film reviews:

> . . . the old invisible-man setup . . . one of those lost-patrol affairs . . .

And three from Wolcott Gibbs's theater reviews:

> Mr. Hammerstein is dealing in basic humor, an extension of the snowball-and-silk-hat principle . . .
>
> . . . Mr. Hart put heroism on a theirs-but-to-do-or-die basis . . .
>
> . . . there is some conversation of a gallant, rueful, and won't-you-sit-down nature . . .

The semicolon also has its special uses. Since it wields several facts into a single event, it is one of the favorite tools of the news digester. Here is John Lardner writing about General Montgomery in *Newsweek*:

> I saw him in Reggio the first day I spent in Italy; saw him 100 miles up the road talking to troops in a wood the next day; and the day after that his car suddenly pulled up 100 yards from my truck at a point 30 miles to the east.

And this is a typical bit from *Time*:

> No V-Day?
>
> Untie those whistles; take those boards off the shop-windows; disband those parades; put that bottle of bourbon back on the shelf—there may be no V-day.
>
> So said the War & Navy Departments last week in an OWI statement: V-day may be spread gradually over days and weeks. No general surrender of the German Armies is expected; they may gradually disintegrate and surrender piecemeal. And the Allies' policy is not to accept surrender from any hastily contrived substitute German Government; the Allies are not looking for any Nazi Badoglio; the war with Germany will be finally over only when all Germany has been occupied, town by town.

Also, semicolons, the short-sentence mortar, are the trademark of a good popularizer. For instance, *Microbe Hunters* by Paul de Kruif literally teems with semicolons. This is the pattern:

> Pasteur started hunting microbes of disease and punched into a boil on the back of the neck of one of his assistants and grew a germ from it and was sure it was the cause of boils; he hurried from these experiments to the hospital to find his chain microbes in the bodies of women dying with child-bed fever; from here he rushed out into the country to discover—but not to prove it precisely—that earthworms carry anthrax bacilli from the deep buried carcasses of cattle to the surface of the fields. . . .
>
> . . . The time for the fatal final test drew near; the very air of the little laboratory became finicky; the taut workers snapped at each other across the Bunsen flames . . .

> . . . One dead child after another Loeffler examined; he poked into every part of each pitiful body; he stained a hundred different slices of every organ; he tried—and quickly succeeded in—growing those queer barred bacilli pure . . .
>
> . . . They went at it frantic to save lives; they groped at it among bizarre butcherings of countless guinea-pigs; in the evenings their laboratories were shambles like the battlefields of old days when soldiers were mangled by spears and pierced by arrows . . .
>
> . . . He shot his mixture into new guinea-pigs; in three days they grew cold; when he laid them on their backs and poked them with his finger they did not budge.

However, not all popularizers agree on this point. One of them, Walter B. Pitkin, the author of *Life Begins at Forty*, always writes extremely short sentences, from six to ten words. Since he despises semicolons, his style reads like this:

> In 1919 I began to work with shell-shocked Army officers who were having a tough time returning to the world of business. Here was one who had broken almost every bone in his body and had lived to resume his old job with hardly any mental upset. Here was another whose injuries were trivial. If he carried a cane he could get around easily. But he loathed the cane. He seemed to regard it as a public confession of weakness. He was forever trying to do without it. Worse yet, he strove to walk without a limp. The strain was terrible. He insisted that life was empty for a cripple. Within two years he killed himself.
>
> I reached two conclusions. Many people are better off with grave handicaps than with trifling ones. The grave handicap releases copious energies. The trifling handicap seems to stir the person too feebly to open up the big valves of nervous and mental power. Then, too, people often try to mask the petty handicap, which leads to further complication of the personality.

Now let's put in semicolons, colons, dashes, and paragraphs:

> In 1919 I began to work with shell-shocked Army officers who were having a tough time returning to the world of business. Here was one who had broken almost every bone in his body and had lived to resume his old job with hardly any mental upset. Here was another whose injuries were trivial: if he carried a cane he could get around easily. But he loathed the cane—he seemed to regard it as a public confession of weakness. He was forever trying to do without it; worse yet, he strove to walk without a limp. The strain was terrible; he insisted that life was empty for a cripple; within two years he killed himself.
>
> I reached two conclusions:
>
> Many people are better off with grave handicaps than with trifling ones: the grave handicap releases copious energies, the trifling handicap seems to stir the person too feebly to open up the big valves of nervous and mental power.
>
> Then, too, people often try to mask the petty handicap, which leads to further complication of the personality.

See the difference?

In fact, without colons and semicolons no-one could imitate spoken language in print. As an example, listen to a little eye-witness-account from a detective story by the British poet Cecil Day Lewis (Nicholas Blake):

> "I knows my way about here in the dark like a mole. I'd a torch, of course; but I didn't want to use it in case it should give away my position to the enemy. A proper night attack—that's what I wanted to spring on the blighter. See? Well, I came upstairs quiet, and just as I rounded the corner at the other end of this passage I saw some one outside the door of Mr. Bunnett's room. There's a bit of light comes in through the skylight just above; not what you'd call light but not as dark as the stairs: just enough for me to see a sort of figure. So I clicks on

my torch: only, me standing close against the wall, the movement hit the torch against it about a second before the light went on: the button's a bit stiff, you see. The blighter heard the sound and it gave him time to nip round the corner and be off; moved like a bleeding streak of lightning, he did. If you'll pardon the expression, just saw his tail light whisking off, as you might say. I goes after him, thinking he'd be bound to run out by the front entrance, but seems like he didn't."

So, punctuation marks are handy gadgets in writing plain language. If you want to, you can even go further and explore the frontiers of punctuation, so to speak: new punctuation marks are always cropping up. Here is one that seems to have a future: figures for enumeration. Of course, figures have always been used in outlines and so on; but nowadays you can watch them becoming a punctuation mark proper. *Time* is an inveterate numberer:

> Britain's adherence to unconditional surrender is based on: 1) the determination to reform and re-educate Germany; 2) the equal determination to avoid any truck whatever with Hitler and his gang; 3) the acceptance of the argument that a war between ideas means a European civil war rather than one between nations . . .
>
> . . . But the Nazis did have the sense to install as their No. 1 puppet a Slovak who commands a real following: a canny, bullet-headed nationalist and priest named Joseph Tiso. With political craft and German aid, Tiso has: 1) fed his countrymen relatively well; 2) provided state jobs; 3) promoted Slovaks in government service; 4) suppressed pro-Czechs, by deporting them or threatening to . . .
>
> . . . Costa Rica's Presidential campaign, so bitter that it threatened civil war, ended last week in a comparatively peaceful election (two were killed in an interior village). The winners: 1) Teodoro Picado, candidate of incumbent President Rafael Calderon Gardia's Republicans and of the Leftist *Vanguardia Popular*; 2) Costa

Rica, which kept its status as the only democracy in dicta tor-ridden Central America . . .

Exercise

Here is, without punctuation, a piece from Leo M. Cherne's *The Rest of Your Life*:

> The United States will not suffer a serious postwar inflation because slowness of reconversion unemployment both business and public uncertainty will work against the dissavings that economists fear so much we wont have inflation because everything that will happen to you will compel you to hold on to your money rather than spend it here is a preview of the kind of deflationary developments that will occur first of all there will be termination unemployment secondly theres the absolute certainty that take home pay will fall youll hold on to your savings much tighter when your weekly pay envelope is thinner and thinner it will be because of the reduction in hours and overtime third youre going to wait for prices to come down wartime conditions forced prices up youll be saying to yourself and youve waited so long you can wait a little longer fourth youll be waiting for the new products that you read about and havent seen in the shop windows why rush out and get a radio when that swell FM television standard short wave combination may be just a few months away fifth and most important theres the basic fact of what the war economy didnt do to you it didnt tighten your belt too uncomfortably and there will be no real pressure for you to slip the strap out of the buckle immediately you haven't been starved enough so that youll want to rush out madly and buy if you had been going without shoes in patched up pants in a cotton overcoat as our allies have been doing then certainly youd let loose in the greatest buying spree of your life but no matter how long the war lasts you wont be brought to desperation furthermore however insufficient our future production you will go into the stores

> and shops certain that you will be able to get all you need for your bodys comfort even if you cant get all you want for your hearts desire no we will not be exclaiming after the war good grief how the money rolls out people will not be letting go instead of a flight from the dollar we will have a desperate clinging to the dollar until employment begins to pick up again and job tenure begins to look more real

Looks like a page from a stream-of-consciousness novel this way, doesn't it? Now translate it into a sane economic argument by punctuating it up to the hilt. Here are the first few lines as a starter:

> The United States *will not suffer* a serious postwar *inflation* because:
>
> (1) slowness of reconversion;
>
> (2) unemployment;
>
> (3) both business and public uncertainty—
>
> will work against the "dis-savings" that economists fear so much.
>
> *We won't have inflation because everything that will happen to you will compel you to hold on to your money rather than spend it.*
>
> Here is a preview of the kind of "*de*-flationary" developments that will occur:
>
> First of all, there will be *termination unemployment* . . .

Chapter XII

TURNABOUT RHETORIC

RHETORIC, says the dictionary, is the art of using words. So, literally, a book on "the art of plain talk" is a book n rhetoric. But, of course, this isn't what we usually mean by hetoric: we mean figures of speech, high-sounding phrases, ıncy business with words. We mean Churchill's speeches: . . . I have nothing to offer but blood, toil, tears and sweat . . Never in the field of human conflict was so much owed y so many to so few . . . We shall fight on the beaches, we ıall fight on the landing grounds, we shall fight in the fields nd in the streets, we shall fight in the hills; we shall never ırrender . . . I have not become the King's First Minister in rder to preside over the liquidation of the British Emire . . ."

Now, this is not plain talk; anybody can see that. So why on't I tell you not to be rhetorical in your speech and writıg, and let it go at that?

The answer is that rhetoric is often hard to tell; some peole use it all the time without knowing it. Two or three hunred years ago, for instance, rhetoric was so natural to writers ıat they used it even when talking about simple language. ı the eighteenth century, Dr. Samuel Johnson, in his preface › Shakespeare's plays, wrote:

> If there be, what I believe there is, in every nation, a style which never becomes obsolete, a certain mode of phraseology so consonant and congenial to the analogy and principles of its respective language as to remain settled and unaltered: this style is probably to be sought

> in the common intercourse of life, among those wh
> speak only to be understood, without ambition or el
> gance.
>
> The polite are always catching modish innovation
> and the learned depart from established forms of speec
> in hope of finding or making better; those who wish fo
> distinction forsake the vulgar, when the vulgar is righ
> but there is a conversation above grossness and below r
> finement, where propriety resides . . .

And a hundred years earlier, Samuel Butler wrote:

> Some writers have the unhappines, or rather Prod
> gious Vanity to affect an obscurity in their Stiles, indevou
> ing by all meanes not to be understood, but rather lik
> witches to cast a mist before the eies of their Reader
> These are Owles of Athens only in avoyding the Ligh
> which they do, not so much in regard of the Profoundn
> of what they deliver, which is commonly very vulgar an
> slight when it is understood, but appeare's very learne
> when it is disguisd in dark and insignificant expression
> To write not to be understood is no less vaine then
> speake not to be heard. Fooles and Madmen use to talk
> to themselves in Publique, and he that publishes th
> which he would have no Man understand but himse
> do's the same thing. These are like Citizens that com
> monly choose the Darkest streets to set up in, or mak
> false lights that the Spots and Steines of their Stuffs ma
> not be perceived. But they have another Marke at whic
> this folly always aymes, and seldom misses of, the A
> miration of the weake and Ignorant, who are apt to co
> temne whatsoever they can understand, and admire an
> thing they cannot.

Nowadays, of course, we don't deliberately write period
(build-up) sentences like the first one in the Samuel Johnso
quotation; we don't fish in Roget's *Thesaurus* for word-pai
like *settled and unaltered*; we don't drag in *witches* or *ow
of Athens* for similes; but we can't escape rhetoric and som

imes even write rhythmic, four-part, climactic sentences like his one. Often our rhetoric is natural and easily understood, ike these samples from Samuel Grafton's column:

> We are clearly riding the express in the far east, whereas in the west we seem, for the time being, to be on a local train.
>
> There is small doubt that this situation will change, for General Eisenhower is not spending the spring in England just so he can go down to Kew in lilac-time . . .
>
> . . . The Russian strategy might be described as one of never letting the enemy settle down in one place for a slugging match; the German soldier in Russia always has a date with battle two hundred miles away, and he is always running to keep it, while holding his trousers up with one hand.

ut more often rhetoric gets in the way of plain talk, as in ıese unconsciously periodic sentences from a movie review:

> Very late—but the film is ready for national release, I am glad to say—I hacked through the thicket of "delightfuls" and "enchantings" which had kept me at a distance, to see "Jeannie," a gently characterized British-made comedy about a Scottish peasant woman who discovers, in the course of a trip to pre-war Vienna, that she doesn't have to feel like an old maid after all. A more acute pointing of the roles of an English business man (Michael Redgrave) and an almost traditional sponging count, more accuracy with the Viennese bourgeoisie (the hotel personnel seems very good), and sets much more evocative in details could have made it an entirely beautiful film. But Barbara Mullen alone (as Jeannie), in her prim, sharp-tuned delicateness, would make it one of the easiest, sweetest of light comedies; and I must apologize for my slowness in agreeing with everyone else who has seen it.

And occasionally the results of rhetoric are disastrous, as in is historical example (from a report in the *New York Times*, .ted Naples, November 28, 1943):

> A meeting in honor of Senator Benedetto Croce toda
> turned into a tumultuous anti-monarchical demonstra
> tion. Senator Croce . . . spoke freely against the king . .
> . . . It was characteristic of the temper of the crow
> . . . that Senator Croce did not find it in agreement wit
> him in his demand for a regency. Those present wante
> to sweep away the entire house of Savoy.
>
> When the Senator asked the rhetorical question, "D
> we want to abolish the monarchy?" the crowd shouted
> "Yes!" Senator Croce, however, tried to say "No" but wa
> drowned out by shouts.

Clearly, if we want to avoid any misunderstanding, the bes thing is not to use any rhetoric whatsoever. In other word we must try *not* to play any games with our words or idea *not* to arrange them in pairs or triplets or quadruplets, an to do no sentence-tightrope-walking. After all, when we ge down to it, rhetoric is nothing else but arranging our word in neat little patterns—either by following a certain rhythn or by keeping the sentence in balanced suspense, or by con paring or contrasting ideas. Often a writer does all this at th same time, as Grafton in the sentence about the express in th east and the local train in the west, or Churchill in the "bloo sweat and tears" sentence. Let's study these examples to lear something about the dangers of rhetoric:

First, is it possible that the reader misses the rhythm these sentences, so that he doesn't get the significance of th arrangement? Let's see: In the Grafton sentence the first ha ("We are clearly riding the express in the far east") is quic and determined, while the second half ("whereas in the we we seem, for the time being, to be on a local train") is slov awkward and hesitant. This checks, of course, with the mea ing of the sentence; but how many of the hurried readers of newspaper column will profit from such a subtle rhetoric device?

How about the rhythm of the famous Churchill quotatio "I have nothing to offer but blood, toil, tears and sweat' Churchill, using a four-part sequence as is his custom, bui he sentence up toward the word "sweat" (the speech was neant to encourage people in their war effort). Result: every-ody now misquotes "blood, sweat and tears," using a differ-nt, three-part rhythm and ending up in the defeatist "tears."

Next, let's test the comparison-and-contrast device. Grafton bviously meant to say that things in Europe are going slow, hings in the East fast. But the metaphor is unexplained otherwise it would be a simile), and so the reader may easily et confused when he sees the naval war in the Pacific com-ared to a train (instead of a ship) and something about a ocal train in Europe, although the point seems to be that in Europe things haven't yet started at all.

The famous Churchill metaphor is even more trouble. First, ll readers and listeners have skipped the "toil" so that there re now three items left; and what they have chiefly in com-non is that they are wet. So the reader gets a vague notion hat Churchill used a little word picture of three wet things nstead of saying *war*; and that's that. Actually, Churchill, in is balanced phrase, described the battlefront (blood), the omefront (toil), the consequences of battle (tears), and the onsequences of homefront toil (sweat), putting them all in hronological and logical order.

The question is, Would it have been better for Grafton to ay "The war in Europe is slow in getting started" and for Churchill, "You must expect great suffering and hard work"? Nobody, of course, can answer such a question: but there is no loubt that the rhetorical versions are more apt to be mis-nderstood than the plain ones. So let's add to our rules for lain talk:

Do not use rhythm. (Maybe your reader won't catch on.)
Do not use periodic sentences.
Do not use rhetorical questions.
Do not use metaphors without an explanation.
Do not use contrasts without an explanation.
Do not use irony. (Half the people won't get it.)

Sounds simple; but do not forget that periodic sentences with the frosting saved up for the end) are bound to crop up n our talk, and that almost every word in the language has been a metaphor sometime. Since most of the more comple: notions are now covered by words that originally—in Latin Greek, etc.—meant simple, everyday things, it's literally tru to say that "our language is a cemetery of dead metaphors." (If you throw all the dead metaphors out of this sentence, i means that "our tongue-use is a sleeping place of dead carry overs.") So we should take those antirhetorical rules for plai talk with a grain of salt (another metaphor) and at least cu down on our rhetoric wherever we can. If you are one of thos people to whom rhetoric comes natural, this will be hard o you; a good and horrible example might help. Here are som excerpts from an article by Philip Wylie in the *Saturday Re view of Literature*:

> From 1929 to 1939 the mood of America was one c disappointment. With the beginning of the war i Europe, it became grievous disappointment. We are nov facing the postwar era in a condition of *abject pre-di: appointment*. Individuals who belong to minorities *shak their heads* about coming persecution . . .

(All the build-up for "abject pre-disappointment"—wha ever that may mean—is canceled out by the wrong-drawe metaphor "shake their heads.")

> . . . *Labor worries* about the hostility of the returnin armies; *soldiers worry* about getting jobs; *the farmer i resigned* to becoming a state charge . . .

(Does that mean that farmers don't worry, or are they resigne in order to avoid using the word *worry* three times?)

> . . . *That detached wizard, the man from Mars,* might b startled by the mood.

(The man from Mars is bound to be detached; but what make him a wizard?)

> He would wonder why we were weeping at the dimin tion of *economic gravy from the "frontier"* . . .

(Oh Pioneers! They were out for gravy.)

> . . . *The wizard from Mars* will find the reason only if he hunts for a psychological answer to the question.

(All right: he is from Mars *and* a wizard.)

> He will find that most Americans are *not men but children.*

(I know it's a metaphor, but what about the women?)

> He will find that their emotional responses to their magnificently implemented present are unluckily founded upon a set of *six-year-old myths* . . .

(He doesn't mean the lies of 1938, he means fairy tales for kids.)

> . . . and proverbs which had the appearance of truth only so long as raw resources were potentially available even to *black sheep ducking* . . .

(Ah! The perfect mixed metaphor at last.)

> . . . *disgrace in Dakota* and *hoboes walking in the wilderness.*

(This looks as if the frontier consisted of two regions: (a) Dakota, a haven for black sheep, and (b) the wilderness, frequented by hoboes.)

> For the literature of America is *entirely* a wishful literature *insofar as* all juvenile and *most adult writing is concerned* . . .

(Well, what is it: entirely or mostly?)

> Now, *the Martian* . . .

(No wizard this time)

> . . . will note that when the *hope* of becoming rich by magic is lost to *a nation of infantile people whose subconscious philosophy is constellated around the mainte-*

> *nance of conditions which will support that hope,* then those people have lost their all—spiritually speaking . . .

(This time, the italics were already there in the original. So the writer *must* have meant that a philosophy can be subconscious, and that such a bunch of formless half-thoughts can be constellated like stars around the maintenance of conditions—or if he didn't mean anything so literal, what *did* he mean by all those italicized metaphors?)

> . . . They have lost their *dream.* They have lost their *direction.* They have lost any *concept of their purpose.*

(It's rhythmical all right, but it sounds rather like an anticlimax.)

> The *dream was* always *an illusion* . . .

(Now it has happened: he explains one metaphor by another one for the same thing. This is what might be called the perfect *Roget's-Thesaurus* sentence. The dream was an illusion; the notion was a whim; the fancy was a myth; the vision was a shadow; the phantom was a chimera . . .)

> *Cinderella is the mother of our debacles.*

(Let's stop here. This goes on and on and on in the same style.)

Now here is your

Exercise

Translate these excerpts into non-rhetorical, matter-of-fact English. Here are the first few sentences as a starter:

> Most of the American people seem disappointed. This mood started with the depression in 1929 and became worse in 1939 when the war in Europe started. It will be still worse after this war. Already members of various groups foresee a letdown . . .

Go on from here and strip all the fancy language to the bone

Chapter XIII

FOLLOW THE LANGUAGE

PLAIN talk is the language of the people. If you follow all the rules you have learned earlier in this book, your peech and writing will become simple and readable and ave the popular touch. Often this will seem unorthodox: If you write for a scientific journal and use the word *babies* nstead of *infants,* some readers may feel uneasy; if you ay *buy* instead of *purchase* in a legal document, your fellow awyers may resent the informality.

Anybody who simplifies his language must do it at the risk f appearing too informal and outspoken. But many may hrink from using what is known as incorrect grammar for he sake of simplicity; you want to be readable, but not purosely illiterate.

But what is correct grammar? Often it is nothing but rules et up by schoolteachers to stop the language from going where t wants to go. English, like all other languages, tends toward implification. Simple language devices are gradually worked ut in popular speech. Naturally, they are different from arlier, more complicated ways of saying the same thing; nd so the grammarians call those new forms incorrect and veryone who uses them, uneducated.

Three hundred years ago the grammarians protested against he new form *its* and against the new passive infinitive formed vith *being*. Today they are fighting against such things as repositions at the end of a sentence, split infinitives, or using *hem* and *their* after indefinite pronouns like *everyone* or *anyody*.

I have talked about the preposition at the end of a sentence on page 89. Now let's find some witnesses for the defense of the split infinitive. They are surprisingly enthusiastic. Professor J. Hubert Jagger, in *English in the Future,* writes:

> There is no doubt that the split infinitive will in the end succeed because of its superiority to any other arrangement of the words in many sentences.

And George Oliver Curme, in his *Syntax,* says simply:

> The split infinitive is an improvement of English expression.

James Thurber, not a philologist, has put it even better:

> Word has somehow got around that the split infinitive is always wrong. This is of a piece with the outworn notion that it is always wrong to strike a lady.

It is not hard to find examples where the split infinitive is the only simple way of saying it. Curme quotes "He failed to entirely comprehend it" and Fowler, in *Modern English Usage,* uses "Our object is to further cement trade relations." Here is one I found in the AP story of MacArthur's landing in the Philippines:

> Striking at a point where he is in position to quickly cut off the Island of Luzon . . . on which Manila is situated, from Mindanao on the South, MacArthur poured supplies ashore . . .

(The publisher's editor found another example on Page 1. of this book. He was against it, but I won.)

It's the same story with *them* and *their* after indefinite pronouns. If possible, the so-called incorrect usage is even firmer established. "In older English the plural was common here," says Curme. And why not? As long as English does not do away with gender, like Hungarian, why not use *their* as a practical makeshift device where neither *his* nor *her* fits. What's wrong with this sentence from Fielding's *Tom Jones*

> Everyone in the house were in their beds.

Or with this one from a speech by President Roosevelt:

> There have always been cheerful idiots in this country who believed that there would be no more war for us, if everybody in America would only return into their homes and lock their front doors behind them.

Or this from a speech by Winston Churchill (on the British policy toward Spain):

> Everyone can have their opinion about that . . .

Even one of our leading literary critics, Edmund Wilson, uses this construction:

> For years I have been hearing about detective stories. Almost everybody I know seems to read them, and they have long conversations about them in which I am unable to take part.

And speaking of detective stories, what would a mystery-story writer do if he had to use *his* or *her,* giving away the murderer's sex for the sake of correct grammar? Or would you rewrite this sentence from a mystery story by Ngaio Marsh?

> Someone came this way between 4:30 and 6 on Monday evening. I hope to learn something of their identity.

So you see that the grammarians' superstitions get in the way when you try to write simple English. In fact, grammar itself gets in the way. The whole system of parts of speech, the mainstay of our grammar books, is slowly being undermined by our modern way of talking, by unclassifiable word groups like *pin-up girl, dollar-a-year man* or *pay-as-you-go tax* or by our habits of *motoring, dating, weekending* and whatnot. We carelessly string words together and use them as verbs, nouns or adjectives to suit ourselves, and leave it to the grammarians to label the proper parts of speech in word groups like *Book Find Club* or *Lost-and-Found Department.* If we just follow the English language and write it unafraid of those new "ungrammatical" forms, our style will naturally be colloquial and casual. Casualness, the light touch, is what makes modern English sound modern. Lots of people seem to think that fashionable words like *Blitzkrieg* or things like college slang or jive talk are the important features of current English. Actually, these new words are unimportant fads. What counts, and what is clearly changing our written language, is the gradual acceptance of casual English in print. Fifty years ago, for instance, the literary technique of using a word and exposing it at the same time was known only to a few. Today it is found even in first books like Thomas R. St. George's *c/o Postmaster,* which opens like this:

> One bright morning, early in the spring of 1942, fifty-seven average young men were routed out of a West Coast barracks at the brutal hour of 5 a. m., pushed into *the semblance of a straight line,* and informed by a captain (who played to the hilt *this reasonable facsimile of a "zero hour"*) that they were on shipment. At least six of the fifty-seven received this *with practically no feeling whatsoever,* having spent the night wallowing in *what passed for vice in Paso Robles, California.* The others had sat around and gloried in such wallowing smoked too much, drunk too many *alleged whiskey cokes,* and come home by special request of the Provost Marshal.

Wolcott Gibbs, the *New Yorker's* theater critic, uses this device habitually:

> Now and then, for purposes not necessary to investigate, the stage gets hold of a pretty good book and, just as Injun Joe knocked off the doctor in the cemetery really murders it. This happened last week when H. Clay Blaney presented *what was said to be a version of "The House in Paris,"* by Elizabeth Bowen. Miss Bowen, in the majority critical opinion, is an honest and sensitive writer. In addition to the work now being burlesqued at the Fulton, she has written "The Hotel" and "The Death of the Heart" and she has even been compared, by *what I suppose are moderately respectable English authorities,* with Katharine Mansfield and Virginia Woolf.

This playing down of words or phrases is what makes the casual style so effective. There are many ways of doing it. There is the I-don't-really-mean-it technique, shown in these two examples, there is the deliberately inaccurate description, the conversational exaggeration, the leaving out of details. Where the heavy-handed, old-fashioned, emphatic writer tries hard to bring out his important points, the casual writer makes them stick in the reader's mind by playing down everything else. In a sentence that reads like this

the old-school writer will concentrate on the peaks and the modern one will work on the valleys. He will use all the devices he knows to just barely touch on minor points, so that the reader will have no trouble getting at the gist of the matter.

It is not hard to find examples of this modern, casual style, if you know where to look for it. A good place is the editorial page of a big newspaper, in the second or third column (after serious policy matters have been taken care of). Here is a typical item that shows well the difference between heavy, scientific treatment and the light, offhand manner:

> BONING UP
>
> There was a nostalgic little item in the New York newspapers the other day . . . One Dr. Harootian, addressing a dental society meeting, told how little capsules of pulverized beef bone, swallowed three times a day for eight days, had reduced the incidence of dental caries among a group of patients . . .
>
> Dr. Harootian seemed convinced that it is the fluorides in the beef bone that does the trick, but he admitted that it might also be the fluorides in combination with some other things, though, of course, the good doctor didn't use such crude and unscientific language as that. What

> he actually said was that "an optimal concentration of several factors in the bone material may be the most significant feature, rather than the fluoride alone." All the same, the hypothesis that the fluorides somehow encourage the tooth enamel to resist oral bacteria seems to have been pretty well established. Thus bones from elderly cows rather than from calves or heifers are being used in the experiments, since the bones of younger animals contain less of the stuff.

The casual style is also the standard formula for the back pages of the literary magazines. Here is a piece from the "Personal and Otherwise" column in *Harper's*:

> The editors have recently learned that, through a not-too-mysterious leak in the magazine's business office, advance proofs of *Harper's* have been finding their way to a remote Army post in the Aleutians, where a young soldier puts them to good use in working up the post radio station's daily news broadcasts. He has quite a job getting material, but what with relayed ticker copy, Morse code news from the States (picked up by radio operators on the island and sent down to him by messenger), an early copy of *Time*, and the advance proofs of *Harper's*, he says he makes out pretty well.

Here you have most of the elements of good modern English in a nutshell: the free combination of short words instead of complex word formations ("puts them to good use in working up"—"He has quite a job getting material, but what with"—"he says he makes out pretty well"); the word-group nouns ("advance proofs"—"Army post"—"post radio station's"—"news broadcasts"—"ticker copy"—"Morse code news"); the "conversational" use of punctuation marks like hyphens and parentheses; and the casual touch ("not-too-mysterious"—"quite a job"—"what with this and that"—"he makes out pretty well").

Now look through an issue of that sophisticated, masterly casual magazine, *The New Yorker:*

THE TALK OF THE TOWN

President Roosevelt reported that the Dumbarton Oaks people had agreed on ninety per cent of the problems before them . . .

A REPORTER AT LARGE

"You'll see what I mean," the brigadier continued. "For example, this opening-of-the-road affair. The idea of the maneuver is that a regiment is going to open up some four miles of road for a truck convoy . . ."

PROFILES

Top commanders must always look at what military men are fond of calling "the big picture." . . .

THE THEATRE

As you may have read somewhere or other, the piece at the Belasco was adapted from a novel of the same name (and by the same hand), which had hell's own success with the ladies who haunt lending libraries . . .

THE CURRENT CINEMA

"To Have and Have Not," the least-known, probably, of recent Hemingway writings, was the one which contrasted certain drunks, cowards, millionaires, and neurotics in and around Key West with a tough and forthright fighting-boat captain, name of Harry Morgan . . .

THE ART GALLERIES

The Newark Museum, being, after all, in Newark, is a little out of the way . . .

MUSICAL EVENTS

. . . the Philharmonic-Symphony opened its hundred-and-third season by featuring Bach and Beethoven before intermission time and serving up three first performances after the lobby-chatter session . . .

THE RACE TRACK

Aqueduct came through the hurricane much bette than Belmont, for, of course, there were practically n fine old trees to blow down . . .

ON AND OFF THE AVENUE

. . . there are deep V-necked cashmere cardigans, whic the figures of our more upholstered ladies cry out for . .

BOOKS

IF THIS BE TREASON, by Margaret Echard (Doubl day, Doran). Readers of current thrillers will not b surprised to find that a panic-stricken young woma named (in this case) Penelope is being followed up an down the West Coast by a mysterious stranger who wea a black patch over one eye, possibly to distinguish hi from all the other men who are in pursuit of apprehe sive young ladies these days. This particular couple en up in Oregon, near a prisoner-of-war camp full of Italian where things get very tough indeed for Penelope, chief because she was once married to an Italian-American w dropped out of sight in Italy in the middle of the wa Some nice, shiny new Oregon scenery, but the rest familiar material.

And now, for a perfect specimen of the casual style, le see how the *New Yorker* presents Hungary in "Our Ov Baedeker." If you look up Hungary, say, in the *Wor Almanac*, you will find:

> Hungary for a thousand years has been the abode of t Magyars. Formerly a kingdom in the Austro-Hungari Empire, it was much reduced in size by the Treaty Trianon (June 4, 1920), losing Transylvania to Ruman Croatia and Batchka to Yugoslavia, as well as Upp Hungary (i.e. Slovakia and Carpatho-Ruthenia) to Czec slovakia . . . etc. etc.

In the *New Yorker*, the same facts are used for this:

The Hungarian language has given the English language very few words—in fact, all we can think of at the moment are "hussar" and "shako." "Goulash" is a German corruption of *gulyas* (pronounced "gooyash"), which means "cowboy," and, by extension, the stew he cooks over his campfire on the Nagy-Alföld, or prairie. Hungary has some of those quaint Central European betrothal customs; for instance, when an unmarried girl goes into the fields with a lunch pail for a harvester she offers him a vase filled with flowers and fruit, and if he accepts it and gives her a lump of sugar they're formally engaged. Practically every Hungarian woman you meet is named Ilona. Suffrage is extended to Hungarian women with rather elaborate restrictions: a woman may vote only if she's over thirty, and then only if she has at least three children, or if she earns an income, or if she has a college degree, or if she's married to a man who has graduated from high school. One out of every four Hungarians is a Calvinist. Ministers of all denominations are paid by the government.

The dominant race in Hungary is the Magyars, a determined people who kept the Holy Kingdom of Hungary geographically intact, except for one interval of a hundred and fifty years, for a thousand years, until, in 1920, two-thirds of it was broken up and parcelled out among Czechoslovakia, Yugoslavia, and Rumania. The trouble with the old kingdom was that, besides Magyars, it contained Germans, Slovaks, Ruthenians, Serbs, Croatians, Jews, Dalmatians, Bosnians, and Illyrians, all of whom were firmly downtrodden by the Magyars. The new setup was ninety-three-per cent Magyar. Central European history and politics are hardly the thing to get started on, so we will simply say the Magyars' contribution to Europe in the Middle Ages was holding back the Turks for several hundred years. The Turks finally got in and dominated the region in and around Hungary for almost two hundred years, and then the Austrians and Poles drove them out and the Austrians took over Hungary.

Under the Hapsburgs there was a good deal of cloak-and-sword stuff which needn't concern us here. Since 1921, Hungary has been a monarchy, with Admiral Horthy as regent, and we needn't bother about him, either.

Hungarians are nuts for paprika, which they sprinkle on everything, or eat just plain. Peasants carry wallets full of paprika, just in case. Other Europeans laugh at the Hungarians because they eat corn on the cob. Another Hungarian delicacy is a stew made of blue trout from Lake Balaton, which is the largest body of fresh water in Central Europe. Budapest, as you doubtless know, is really two cities, joined together by bridges over the Danube. Buda is the older, Pest the newer and smarter. If you want to be fancy, like a radio announcer, the proper pronunciation is Buda*pesht*. Budapest is a great place for boating and crew racing, and the waiters are polite there. Vilma Banky, Ferenc Molnar, and Alexander Korda are Hungarians, and Houdini was of Hungarian descent.

Writing about factual material in this modern, casual fashion is a tough assignment. Just to see how it feels, try your hand at the following

EXERCISE

Here is a key passage from Herbert Spencer's justly famou essay *The Philosophy of Style*, written in 1852:

> On seeking for some clue to the law underlying thes current maxims, we may see shadowed forth in many o them, the importance of economizing the reader's o hearer's attention. To so present ideas that they may b apprehended with the least possible mental effort, is th desideratum toward which most of the rules above quote point. When we condemn writing that is wordy, or con fused, or intricate—when we praise this style as eas and blame that as fatiguing, we consciously or uncor sciously assume this desideratum as our standard of juds

ment. Regarding language as an apparatus of symbols for the conveyance of thought, we may say that, as in a mechanical apparatus, the more simple and the better arranged its parts, the greater will be the effect produced. In either case, whatever force is absorbed by the machine is deducted from the result. A reader or listener has at each moment but a limited amount of mental power available. To recognize and interpret the symbols presented to him, requires part of this power; to arrange and combine the images suggested requires a further part; and only that part which remains can be used for realizing the thought conveyed. Hence, the more time and attention it takes to receive and understand each sentence, the less time and attention can be given to the contained idea; and the less vividly will that idea be conceived.

Now let's rewrite this, using the modern light touch:

> What all these current theories boil down to is giving the reader or hearer less work to do. (Most of them, it seems, are awfully lazy fellows.) In fact, practically all our talk about literary style goes back to the question, Why did I have to work so hard to read the darn stuff? . . .

Go on from here, and apply Spencer's theories to his own style.

Chapter XIV

SHORT CUTS

MOST people seem to think that simplicity and brevity are the same thing, or at least that they must always be together like Siamese twins. That's a superstition: plain talk can be slow and roundabout, and short, condensed sentences are often tough to read. The truth is that there are lots of different types of brevity: some make it easier and some harder.

There is no doubt, of course, that the laconic, epigrammatic style has often great simplicity. Here are, for instance, a few sentences from Bacon's essay *Of Studies*:

> Read not to contradict and confute; nor to believe and take for granted; nor to find talk and discourse; but to weigh and consider. Some books are to be tasted others to be swallowed, and some few to be chewed and digested: that is, some books are to be read only in part others to be read, but not curiously; and some few to be read wholly, and with diligence and attention. Some books also may be read by deputy, and extracts made of them by others; but that would be only in the less important arguments, and the meaner sort of books; else distilled books are like common distilled waters, flashy things.

Nowadays, a large number of writers are paid for bein laconic seven days in the week: I mean the headline writer There is just so much space at the top of a column, and good copyreader is a master in the art of saving words an letters. Often, of course, he gets into headlinese instead plain English, and writes

SECRET BARED

where in conversation he would say, "We've been told a secret." But in general, the headline writer is being forced to rediscover simple English, like this

MUSEUM REGAINS TREASURES IT HID

Sometimes a headline tells the story with a bang, as this one (from the Washington *Daily News*, August 10, 1944):

YANKS AS NEAR PARIS
AS BALTIMORE IS
TO WASHINGTON

Sometimes the headline is by far the best part of the story, as this one (from the *New York Times*):

SHORTS WON'T STAY UP BUT PRICE DOES,
OPA CHARGES IN $300,000 DAMAGE SUIT

If you abbreviate not only sentences but words, headlinese becomes *Variety*ese. You have probably heard about that all-ime high

STIX NIX HIX PIX

which meant, to seasoned *Variety* readers, that small-town moviegoers disliked rural pictures. But this is just a spectacu-ar example of the usual *Variety* headline. Here are some others:

WAR TRIMS PIX FANS

HOT MARGIE HART ADS GET FROWN FROM HAYS

WEBMEN AT SCHOOL CONFAB

This means: Networks are represented at the School Broad-ast Conference.)

BIG BIZ SOFTENS COMPETISH; SIX B'WAY STAGE
SHOWS ALL OK B.O.

And, speaking of box office, this is a typical headline from *'ariety's* box-office page:

'CASA' TERRIF \$32,000, HUB; 'HARVEST' HOT 40G, 3D, 'FRANKENSTEIN' RECORD 8G

This is where *Variety*ese gets into the field of unintelligible abbreviations—unintelligible, that is, to outsiders who are not members of the clan. This kind of language crops up wherever people form a special-interest group. As the *New Yorker* puts it:

> There are circles in which some significance might be attached to the message "86$\frac{1}{8}$ 77$\frac{3}{4}$ Chrysler Cp 1 $\frac{1}{2}$e xd 68 85$\frac{3}{8}$ 84 84$\frac{1}{2}$-$\frac{3}{8}$," which happens to be a New York Stock Exchange quotation. There are other circles in which the following information might be considered important: "May 11-44 1 C.D. 3-4 1:12-4/5 ft 77f 118 8 86$\frac{1}{4}$ 56$\frac{1}{2}$ 46$\frac{1}{4}$ Scurl'kD10 1250 80 Miss Tipper 10 Sergt. Bill 118 V'a Joe 12." This happens to be a fragment of the history of a horse named Blue Valley, as told in the language of *Daily Racing Form.*

Doubtless this language is handy for movie people, stock brokers, horse players, and so on. And obviously, it is *not* plain talk. The apostles for brevity will admit that; they will even admit that the condensed, abbreviated language of, say, *Psychological Abstracts* is far from simple. But somehow when the same condensation principle is applied to current affairs or business news, as in weekly digests or newsletters, they seem to think that that's simple, just because *they* know what it's all about. Take, for instance, this condensed piece of news:

> Expert opinion insists that disaster in Latin America can be avoided only by: economic sanctions against Argentina, with Britain cooperating (based on new agreements for postwar markets), cleaning out all pro-Franco elements, and immediate aid to relieve inflation. Long-range planning for industrialization with long-term credit financing, decent wage guarantees, protection of national interests and equal participation of *domestic* and foreign capital.

To translate all these big words, like *inflation, industrialization, long-term credit financing,* into plain English, would take lots and lots of one- and two-syllable words. Simplification here would mean lengthening instead of shortening.

So we see that true brevity is fine, but that abbreviation and condensation are liable to make things difficult for outsiders. And that's about all you have to know about this business of language short cuts, except for those "flashy things" Francis Bacon talks about, the "extracts" and "distilled books": in other words, the *Reader's Digest* and all those other so-called digests that are so popular nowadays. Actually, the word *digest* is a misnomer: *Reader's Digest* pieces are not digested, that is, rewritten in condensed form; they are cut. And this brings us to the interesting question: Are *Reader's Digest* articles easier to read than the originals?

Offhand, most people would probably say yes. Digest articles are shorter, and they give you the feeling that tedious details have been left out. In fact, they mostly have been; but often hose cut portions are just conversational repetitions and side emarks, the in-between space between important ideas I was alking about in Chapter III—and such articles are not simplified by cutting but are made flavorless and textbooky. This is an important thing for you to know, and it will take a whole article and its *Reader's Digest* version to make the oint. So I am going to reprint here an article that fits into his chapter anyway, first the way it appeared originally in the *New York Times Magazine*, and then the way it was reprinted in the *Digest*. It is called

THE CASE AGAINST 'GOBBLEDYGOOK'

By Maury Maverick

Just before Pearl Harbor, I, newly come to Washington as a civil service employe, was sent to a committee to consider the rights of consumers in his purchase of goods. There I got my baptism under "gobbledygook" which I will try to explain.

First, the word: it is long, sounds foreign, has four

stories. You walk up without benefit of elevator. Second, its definition: talk or writing which is long, pompous, vague, involved, usually with Latinized words. It is also talk or writing which is merely long, even though the words are fairly simple, with repetition over and over again, all of which could have been said in a few words.

Now back to the banks of the Potomac and the meeting I attended. Our chairman, a mild-mannered, amiable-looking fellow, opened as follows:

"We * * *" (long talk with no relation to the subject) * * * "face profound changes in our economic system." (He didn't explain the profundities, or what to do about them.) These, he said "* * * inevitably spring from a broad frame of related and unrelated factors." Then: "Optimum production * * * maladjustments, co-extensive with problem areas * * * alternative, but nevertheless meaningful minimae * * * must be correlation * * * conservation of human and natural resources * * * utilization of factors which in a dynamic democracy can b channelized into both quantitative and qualitativ phases." Toward the end: "We will have informal discussion, evaluating * * * making dynamic" (repeate several times) * * * "in an ad hoc manner, according t the panel concept."

My next chair neighbor was squirming and getting re in the face. He had come a long way across America t attend this "ad hoc"—whatever that is—meeting. "Tha fellow," he whispered angrily, "must be a Communist. The presiding officer interested me in spite of my bor dom, so I made pains to find out what he really was. H was no Communist. But he had consorted so long an intimately with a lot of others like himself that he didn know how to talk plain English. He had become a Tw Gun Word Bandit.

I soon began to realize that the users of Latin phras and big words, the double-talkers and long-winde writers, were moving in on us like an invisible empir In their wake they were creating confusion, dullness an slow down. They were erecting a tyranny the like of which America had never suffered before.

All this has been burning me up for more than two years. Previously, as head of Latin phrases and big words, the Production Board, I had to get information for and from cities. My boys made up a questionnaire 150 pages long. I revolted, but the boys told me there was no other way, and tried to shame me in my country-boy ignorance. How, they said, looking down their noses at me, do *you* know this is wrong?

"Because," I replied smugly, "I was once a Mayor. And if that came into my office I would take one look at the bulk and throw it violently in the waste basket." So we cut it 80 per cent.

As a result, enough cities answered for us to get accurate and helpful statistics. Had we sent the long one, it would never have been answered. Had it been answered, it would never have been completed. Its sheer dead weight would have killed off my entire office force.

Recently, when I became chairman of the Smaller War Plants Corporation, torrents, yea, verily, tidal waves of papers, documents, memoranda, clippings and letters, swirled around me. I was drowning. Thus came my second revolt. In righteous indignation I rattled off a memorandum denouncing gobbledygook language.

People asked me how I got the word. I do not know. It must have come in a vision. Perhaps I was thinking of the old bearded turkey gobbler back in Texas who was always gobbledygobbling and strutting with ridiculous pomposity. At the end of his gobble there was a sort of gook.

The response to the memorandum was immediate and widespread. Letters poured in showing that the American people are tired of double-talk and talk they can't understand. No one regarded the tyranny of words as funny. I was even asked to write this story about it, and I do so in deadly earnestness.

Frequently, I get a memo under a subject entitled, say, "Labor." After reading the four-page memorandum through the third page I begin to realize the subject is not labor at all. The writer is arguing for civilian production in certain areas because labor and materials are available. Why not, then, make the subject "Resumption of civilian production is possible in some areas because * * *" Too long? No. You don't have to read through three pages of double-talk to find out the subject. And, as I said in my gobbledygook memo, make the point and the conclusion in the first paragraph if at all possible. Do it like a well-written newspaper story with headline and all in the beginning.

This is serious and necessary. An executive comes to work. People are waiting to see him. Letters (and memoranda) lie on his desk. He must leave for a wearisome committee meeting at 11, the telephone is ringing, there are unanswered calls, he has to eat lunch with Jones who has flown in from Los Angeles (you can't say no to anybody from L. A.), get back to see a committee from Chicago, administrative procedures must be correlated before he leaves, and finally home, to pass out. (This sentence, like this executive's day, is too long and complicated.)

Memos should be short and to the point. If the executive has to struggle through tiresome, wordy memoranda on his desk, they pile as high as the sky, creating a Great Slow Down Wall. Sometimes the job is never done, memos being written until the problem blows up in your face. Then it is too much and too late.

The Gobbledygookers are forever talking about "levels" of government, as though the Federal Government, for which they work, is in the High Place. This psychological attitude is arrogant, to say the least. It is as if they were a set of oracles or Panchhan Lamas sitting on top of the Tibet Mountains in their monasteries talking (nonsense) to the common people 7,000 feet below.

One memorandum I received was to establish a national policy. It started out by saying that policy should be established "at the Federal level, and appropriately transmitted by directive down to the local level." There followed such words as "celerity," "realistic justification," "procedure and policy difficulties," "categorical denunciation of racial discrimination," "the strategy of this approach is to transfer the issue from one as to the instability of policy in the agency, to a fairly academic issue of whether the management practice of the personnel office is proper."

Consider the misused and wasted words! A justification is no justification unless it is realistic. If you are going to denounce something and intend to do a good job of it, then your denunciation is categorical. Somehow I get the idea that such writing is just an attempt to impress the reader or the boss with the writer's learning.

What is it that brings on this long-winded, heart-breaking wordiness? I'm not sure but I have a hunch that a writer, feeling defeat in advance, gets lengthy and vague in self-defense. If defeat comes, he can hide behind the big words and ascribe it to the ignorance of the people addressed.

Gobbledygook means not only big foolish words but also wasted words. In practically every government order there is a long paragraph pretending to rehash in advance the reasons for the order. Let me quote one and then show how it could be written in short language:

> Whereas, national defense requirements have created a shortage of corundum (as hereafter defined) for the combined needs of defense and private account, and the supply of corundum now is and will be insufficient for defense and essential civilian requirements, unless the supply of corundum is conserved and its use in certain products manufactured for civilian use is curtailed; and it is necessary in the public interest and to promote the defense of the United States, to conserve the supply and direct the distribution and use thereof. Now, therefore, it is hereby ordered that . . .

It could have been written:

"National defense requirements have created a shortage of corundum. This order is necessary to conserve the supply for war and civilian uses, and . . ."

Now let me quote a typical paragraph from a recent order. If you can read it once and know what it means you are a genius:

> For the purposes of subparagraph (1) of this paragraph [gobbledygook, gobbledygook], if a farmer-producer has a maximum [the highest] price for a given class of sales or deliveries of a given variety and kind of vegetable seed, but not for another class of sales or deliveries thereof, he shall determine his maximum price for such latter class of sales or deliveries by adding to or subtracting from his maximum price for the class of sales and deliveries for which he has an established maximum price hereunder the premium or discount, as the case may be, in dollars and cents normal to the trade during said base period for the class of sales or deliveries to be priced in relation to said class of sales or deliveries for which he has an established maximum price hereunder; and the resultant figure shall be his maximum price for the class of sales and deliveries in question.

Then there is a certain Government report nearly 700 pages long. Had it been put in 100 pages of plain English, with its constant repetitions cut out, it would have been a valuable contribution to our country. But the people who worked on it worked with each other, talked to each other, and lived with each other for more than a year. When the report came out, they had developed a new lingo of their own. It was Choctaw. It was quintuple-talk, none of the quintuplets being identical.

Here is some of it, neither the best nor the worst, but average:

> Yet, in view of the extent of unmet need, it is unfortunate that these additional funds were devoted solely to a measure making payments to a group in relatively less need, or that, granted the effectiveness of Federal financial inducements in calling forth additional State and local moneys, these induce-

> ments were not also available for the program meeting the most urgent needs of large numbers—general relief. . . .
>
> This problem of coordinating public aid programs both horizontally in terms of agency relationships at any one level of government and vertically as between agencies of the Federal, State and local governments, is likely to challenge administrative ingenuity over a long period. [And so it will, brethren.]

These are only two examples. Ye gods! Imagine 700 pages of this kind of reading with the same thing said over and over again!

But I have complained long enough. What are we going to do about it? Well, we might start by applying the following rules:

(1) Make up a Gobbledygook Dictionary, and make it unpopular to use any word on the list.

(2) Try to keep sentences under twenty words, certainly under twenty-five words.

(3) Don't make the memo a sermon or prolonged lecture or a display of "book learning."

(4) Use the telephone for a short conversation if the other fellow isn't too busy, and not a crab.

The worst thing is that our officialdom drags this invisible empire of word death-traps into the press. Newspaper men tear their hair because they have to translate the handouts—if they can. I have heard people curse the Congressional Record. But compared to the Federal Register, which has all official Government orders and regulations, the Record is a miracle of clearness and brevity.

This is certain: If we do all these things we can save time, paper, hours of unnecessary work, our dispositions and, I believe, blood. There must be a new language development in America which will rescue our present language from the curse of confusion. We must stop dragging in the corpses of dead languages. A man's language is a very important part of his conduct. He should be held morally responsible for his words just as he is accountable for his other acts.

Let us be orderly in our language and brief. Slovenly disorder in speech and writing is not only a reflection upon the person's thinking but an insult to the person to whom it is sent.

Plain and simple speech appeals to everyone because it indicates clear thought and honest motives. Here is the point: Anyone who is thinking clearly and honestly can express his thoughts in words which are understandable, and in very few of them. Let's write for the reader and not for ourselves. Make the writing do what it is intended to.

This, after all, should be a crusade in America. I didn't, when I wrote in honest rage about gobbledygook talk, want to be funny, and no one took it that way. One man wrote me from way up in British Columbia and told me of his youth in England. He quoted this passage from "Alice in Wonderland":

"Speak English," said the Eaglet. "I don't know the meaning of half these long words, and what's more, I don't believe you do, either."

And I will close with a text from the Bible, which was sent me by a minister. It reads: "Except ye utter by the tongues, words easy to be understood, how shall it be known what is spoken . . . for ye shall speak into the air."

And now read the *Reader's Digest* version:

THE CURSE OF GOBBLEDYGOOK

> Except ye utter by the tongue words easy to be understood, how shall it be known what is spoken? For ye shall speak into the air.
>
> —I Corinthians XIV:9

Condensed from the New York Times Magazine

Maury Maverick

Former Congressman from Texas; now Chairman of the Smaller War Plants Corporation

In Washington, just before Pearl Harbor, I got my baptism under "gobbledygook." I was sent to a committee meeting at which the chairman spoke at length of "maladjustments co-extensive with problem areas . . . alternative but nevertheless meaningful minimae . . . utilization of factors which in a dynamic democracy can be channelized into both quantitative and qualitative phases . . ."

Our chairman was a mild-mannered, amiable-looking fellow, who had consorted so long with a lot of others like himself that he didn't know how to talk plain English. He talked gobbledygook.

People ask me where I got "gobbledygook." Perhaps I was thinking of the old turkey gobbler back in Texas who was always gobbledygobbling and strutting with ridiculous pomposity. At the end of his gobble there was a sort of gook.

In Washington I soon realized that the double-talkers and long-winded writers were moving in on us, creating in their wake confusion, dullness and slowdown. For instance, in practically every government order there is a long paragraph pretending to rehash in advance the reasons for the order. Let me quote one and then show how it could be written in short language:

> Whereas, national defense requirements have created a shortage of corundum (as hereafter defined) for the combined needs of defense and private account, and the supply of corundum now is and will be insufficient for defense and essential civilian requirements, unless the supply of corundum is conserved and its use in certain products manufactured for civilian use is curtailed; and it is necessary in the public interest and to promote the defense of the United States, to conserve the supply and direct the distribution and use thereof. Now, therefore, it is hereby ordered that . . .

It could have been written:

> National defense requirements have created a shortage of corundum. This order is necessary to conserve the supply for war and essential civilian use, and . . .

Here is a typical paragraph from a recent order. If you can read it once and know what it means you are a genius:

> For the purposes of subparagraph (1) of this paragraph, if a farmer-producer has a maximum price for a given class of sales or deliveries of a given variety and kind of vegetable seed, but not for another class of sales or deliveries thereof he shall determine his maximum price for such latter class of sales or deliveries by adding to or subtracting from his maxi mum price for the class of sales and deliveries for which he has an established maximum price hereunder the premium or discount, as the case may be, in dollars and cents normal to the trade during said base period, for the class of sales o deliveries to be priced in relation to said class of sales o deliveries for which he has an established maximum pric hereunder; and the resultant figure shall be his maximum price for the class of sales and deliveries in question.

What is it that brings on this long-winded, heartbreak ing wordiness? I have a hunch that a writer, feeling defea in advance, gets lengthy and vague in self-defense. Ther if defeat comes, he can ascribe it to the ignorance of th people addressed.

Somehow I get the idea that gobbledygook writing just an attempt to impress the reader or the boss with th writer's learning.

The American people are tired of double-talk and tal they can't understand. What are we going to do about i Well, memos should be short and to the point. If th executive has to struggle through tiresome, wordy mem randa, they pile high on his desk, creating a Great Slow down Wall. We might start by applying the followir rules:

1. Make it unpopular to use gobbledygook words.
2. Try to keep sentences under 20 words, certain under 25 words.
3. Don't make a display of "book learning."

If we do these things we can save time, paper, hours unnecessary work and our dispositions. Our present la guage must be rescued from the curse of confusion.

> A man's language is an important part of his conduct. He should be held morally responsible for his words just as he is accountable for his other acts. Let us be orderly and brief. Slovenly disorder in speech and writing is not only a reflection upon a person's thinking but an insult to the person addressed. Anyone who is thinking clearly and honestly can express his thoughts in words which are understandable, and in very few of them.

I certainly agree with Mr. Maverick that it's good to be rief; but I think it's clear that the abbreviation of his own rticle is not an improvement or a simplification. The *Digest* hanged hardly a word of Mr. Maverick's style; but it cut way two-thirds of the original (735 as against 2,269 words) nd robbed it of its rambling, easygoing, conversational tone. he shorter version still makes all the essential points, but it nakes a little exhortation out of an explosion.

As you see, a *Reader's Digest* "condensation" is an intricate ob of cutting and reassembling, done with great skill. The et effect, in this particular case, is to cut the reading time by wo-thirds (which is a measurable advantage for people who on't have much time to spend on reading), but to leave the eading effort needed just about where it was: Tested by our ardstick formula, the original article (without the quotes) ates STANDARD (3.3) and the short version the same (3.4). In ther words, this article already had the STANDARD readbility that is the norm for the *Reader's Digest*, so that there as no gain in leaving out any difficult portions. On the conrary, what was left out was the personal touches and the andom flow of ideas that made the original so interesting and eadable. But that doesn't mean, of course, that it should not ave been cut; after all, it gives you the gist of Mr. Maverick's leas in a jiffy.

EXERCISE

Study the two versions closely and compare them sentence y sentence.

Chapter XV

TALKING DOWN AND READING UP

SUPPOSE you are the perfect reader of this book. Yo have read carefully every word I wrote up to this poin you have studied all the examples, you have worked all th exercises. You are thoroughly conscious by now of what mak for simplicity. You measure your sentences, count your affixe and bring in people wherever you can. You know how to u the yardstick formula and are master of the little tricks using verbs or avoiding commenting adjectives and emp words. You have learned how to be neither rhetorical n pedantic. In short, you got the theory of plain talk cold. No you want to practice.

To do that, you want to know where to find VERY EASY En lish, EASY English, FAIRLY EASY English, and so on up t scale, and what kind of language to use for what kind people.

Now, of course, it's impossible to test with our formu everybody's speech, reading, and writing; even to take a so of Gallup poll would be a terrific job. But we can try to ma a guess by playing with a few statistics.

You probably wondered back in Chapter VII how the yar stick formula was worked out. This is not the place for detailed explanation; briefly, it is a way of grading materi for school children. (It goes back to reading lessons on whi children in various grades were tested.) So, if you test a pie of writing and come out with a score of, say, 3.4 (STANDAR you can translate this into school grades and say, This is ea to understand for children in eighth or ninth grade. Here the whole table:

VERY EASY	(0-1)	will be understood in	5th grade
EASY	(1-2)	" " " "	6th grade
FAIRLY EASY	(2-3)	" " " "	7th grade
STANDARD	(3-4)	" " " "	8th and 9th grade (high school freshman)
FAIRLY DIFFICULT	(4-5)	" " " "	10th to 12th grade (high school sophomore to senior)
DIFFICULT	(5-6)	" " " "	college
VERY DIFFICULT	(6 and up)	" " "	by college graduates

Naturally, if you are interested in an adult audience rather than children and adolescents, you will want to know how much education your readers or listeners have had. This does not mean that a person's understanding of reading matter depends solely on the time he spent in school when he was young. But in general, nowadays, a person's education has a great deal to do with the kind of job he can get, the kind of people he meets, the kind of life he lives on the whole, and, of course, his reading and speaking habits. So let's see what the census statistics tell us about "school years completed":

AMONG AMERICANS OVER 25 YEARS

about 90%	have completed	4th grade
about 86%	" "	5th grade
about 80%	" "	6th grade
about 75%	" "	7th or 8th grade
about 40%	" "	1 to 3 years of high school
about 24%	" "	4 years of high school or 1 to 3 years of college
about 4½%	" "	4 years of college

(About 14% of our population are what is called functionally illiterate. The average of "school years completed" is 8.4.)

Now look at this table closely and see how it answers our questions. Every literate person, we see, can read VERY EASY English; and almost everyone can read EASY and FAIRLY EASY English. Three-quarters of the American people—those with an average education—can be expected to understand STAND ARD English (that's why I called it that). Then comes a grea break in the figures and only two-fifths are still with us wher we use FAIRLY DIFFICULT language; only one-fourth can readil understand DIFFICULT English. And only one-twentieth ge the full meaning out of VERY DIFFICULT language. Let's put i this way: Really scientific or academic prose is the idiom o only a few; with some degree of popularization it is possible t reach a large minority; but only STANDARD—that is, conversa tional—English will be fully understood by the averag person.

But that's only half the answer. People don't really like t read things they can just barely understand; they prefer read ing matter where they don't even feel any effort in reading So the average American, perfectly well equipped to rea STANDARD books and magazines, likes stories such as those i the *Saturday Evening Post,* which are, on the average, FAIRL EASY; and the college graduate who could, if he would, spen his time with the *Scientific Monthly* and Thomas Mann, sub scribes to, say, *Time* or the *New Yorker* and reads the Book of-the-Month Club choices. In other words, if we tried to fin what books and magazines people not only can, but do rea at each level, we would have to go about one notch down th scale. For instance, let's look at the difficulty of magazines:

VERY EASY	(0-1):	Comics
EASY	(1-2):	Pulp magazine fiction (confessiona detective, Western)
FAIRLY EASY	(2-3):	Slick-paper magazine fiction (famil and women's)
STANDARD	(3-4):	Slick-paper magazine articles an digest magazines
FAIRLY DIFFICULT	(4-5):	Literary and quality magazines
DIFFICULT	(5-6):	Academic journals and quarterlies
VERY DIFFICULT	(6 or more):	Scientific and professional journa

Thanks to research, it is pretty well known who reads wha kind of magazines. Most people who are fully able to rea FAIRLY EASY magazines such as *Collier's* or the *Saturday Eve ning Post,* consider them as distinctly highbrow and stick t

True Story or the comics; most of those who could deal with the *Reader's Digest* never go higher than *Redbook* or *Cosmopolitan*; most of the potential readers of *Harper's* and the *Atlantic* are content with *Reader's Digest* or *Ladies' Home Journal* articles; and so it goes.

When it comes to a listening audience, this principle of shooting below your target is even more important. As everybody knows, it is harder to follow a difficult lecture than to read the same thing in a book (where you can check back if you didn't quite get what you read). So, it is impractical to present DIFFICULT or even FAIRLY DIFFICULT prose to the ear rather than the eye, and that's why it is hardly ever done in commercial radio. The average radio program is EASY or FAIRLY EASY; and the typical daytime serial (soap opera) is VERY EASY. Even the most highbrow radio programs, e.g. *Invitation to Learning*, are spoken in prose of STANDARD difficulty. (That's why these broadcasts are so readable when they get into print.) The reason is, of course, that a good broadcast has to sound like colloquial prose; and the difference between STANDARD and FAIRLY DIFFICULT language is exactly that between colloquial and bookish English.

So, to reach an audience at a certain level of reading or listening, you not only have to talk the kind of language they will be able to understand without effort, but ordinarily you have to go one step below that level to be sure your ideas will get across. That's an important principle, but let me add one thing quickly: I am talking about levels of reading ability, or language experience, or whatever you want to call it; I am *not* talking about levels of intelligence. This is where most amateur popularizers go wrong; they think they have to talk down. (Webster defines talking down as "simplifying or adapting one's discourse for a lower level of intelligence.") People are not just plain dumb; they may have little book learning, but they usually have a great deal of sense. For instance, they have sense enough to resent empty phrases, to laugh at phony stories, and to recognize folksiness as a fake.

Talking down is hard to describe or define. Here are a few examples:

From a popular-psychology magazine article:

> Strange as it may seem, our moral standards and concepts are based upon our ability to mix and to get along with other people. Any other attitude is antisocial. Self-interest—selfishness, in short—should never trespass upon the rights of others or go so far as to take from others what is their rightful due. Actually, to be unselfish is to be social; to be social, to feel you fit in and are acceptable to the group in which you live, is to be happy.

From a steel company ad:

> (A farmer-boy soldier returns from the war and says:) . . . I don't expect much, now that I'm back. But what I do ask for I really want. I want an honest chance to make a decent living, and to own my own farm some day. If I've got what it takes, I don't want anyone holding me down with needless interference. I've seen too much of slaves . . . I want to worship as I please. I want to say what I think, and not what someone else makes me say. I want to come back to a country where there is competition and fair play and *opportunity*. When I have my own farm, I want to run it *my* way. I don't want anyone else doing my own planning and bossing for me. I guess what I want all adds up to the right to live my own life in my own way—like an *American* . . .

From a government pamphlet:

> For example, a landlord we will call Mr. Jones registered his six-room house at 1004 Dash Street as renting for $85. The Director . . . called Mr. Jones' attention to the fact that he was charging more than the Maximum Rent . . . Mr. Jones registered a complaint as to the proposed reduction—and the Director produced records showing other rentals in the neighborhood. There it all was in black and white . . . Mr. Jones began to see how Rent Control worked. He was not lacking in honesty—nor in patriotism—he just hadn't understood. Once the

regulations were clear in his mind, he willingly agreed to a reduction and the maximum rent became $60.

For contrast, here are two examples of simplifying without talking down. This is how Stuart Chase solves the problem of making an average situation sound real:

> The veterans will be coming back to Main Street to enjoy the peace . . . What will they find? Main Street will not look so different . . . There is Ed's garage, and the First National Bank, and the Palace Theater, and a fine new coat of paint on the Methodist church. Terry's meat market has gone out of business, but there is a new grocery store by the traffic light . . . The town folks will go wild when the young men come back. They will put on a parade and a carnival and fire off the Civil War cannon in Prospect Park, the way they did in 1918. Senator Williamson will make a speech about peace . . .

And this is the beginning of the excellent pocket guide to Great Britain which the War Department prepared for American soldiers:

> You are going to Great Britain as part of an Allied offensive—to beat Hitler. For the time being you will be Britain's guest.
>
> America and Britain are allies. Hitler knows that they are both powerful countries, tough and resourceful. He knows that they, with the other United Nations, mean his crushing defeat in the end. Therefore the first duty of Hitler's propaganda chiefs is to spread distrust between them. If they can do that, Hitler's chance of winning might return.
>
> If you come from an Irish-American family you may think of the English as persecutors of the Irish. Or you may think of them as fighting against us in the Revolution and the War of 1812. But there is no time today to bring up old grievances. We don't worry about which side our grandfathers fought on in the Civil War, because it doesn't mean anything now.

This doesn't underrate anybody's intelligence, and it's admirably simple. It's the style books for the average American ought to be written in and never are. Instead, the nonfiction shelves of our libraries are full of difficult, bookish books that make for slow reading.

If you have had trouble working your way through books on postwar economics, geopolitics or whatnot, don't worry. Most people have. And anyway, it's just a question of word-and-sentence experience and not, as I said, of intelligence. You can get this word-and-sentence experience simply by reading up on whatever subject you are interested in—and I mean reading up: from the STANDARD books to the FAIRLY DIFFICULT books, from the FAIRLY DIFFICULT to the DIFFICULT, and from the DIFFICULT to the VERY DIFFICULT. But don't fool yourself: just reading words doesn't mean understanding. You are only up to a given reading level if you can translate everything on that level down to STANDARD prose, that is, to the form in which you would explain the thing in ordinary conversation. That's not easy: in fact, it is the toughest reading test anybody could devise. But if you do it from time to time, you will get twice as much out of everything you read—you will work harder at reading, but it will pay dividends.

And if you become a word-and-sentence expert in this fashion, don't think that this makes you smarter than other people and gives you the right to talk down to them.

Chapter XVI

CAN SCIENCE BE EXPLAINED?

WHEN people talk about something that's difficult to read, they are apt to say it's "too technical." The ordinary person, when he gets bogged down in a book or article, wouldn't think of saying, "The author of this can't write"; he will say, "A layman like me will never understand this" and let it go at that. In other words, most people think that some subjects are easy and some difficult and it hardly matters what language is used in explaining them.

I don't agree with those people. The principles of simple language are just as important, or maybe more so, in explaining, say, biochemistry, than they are for a news broadcast. The only difference is this: When you use simple language for anything that is *not* scientific or technical, you can explain it to anybody; but when you simplify science, you will find that only part of it will be understandable to the layman, and another part, however simply stated, will be clear only to people who have some training in that branch of science. There is no scientific discovery or theory that cannot be popularized—up to a point; the important thing is to know just what can be explained to the ordinary person and what can't.

Let me show you an example of what I mean: Some time ago Commander Howard S. Aiken of Harvard University developed a so-called mathematical robot, that is, an automatic calculator that can solve tremendous, otherwise insoluble mathematical problems. Now how can anybody explain this incredible machine to a layman? At first sight, you would think it's impossible; but that isn't so. In fact, the machine is being operated by laymen; they get a code book prepared by a mathematician and all they have to do is to follow the code and punch holes in a tape. So the *operations* of the machine can be explained very simply; the book probably says something like "First punch hole A6; then punch hole C31" and so on.

But you can also go one step further and explain to a layman what Commander Aiken was about when he was building that machine: you can tell what the problem was, for what purpose the machine was going to be used, what theory he had in mind and how he put it into practice, and finally what tests he used to be sure the monster-gadget worked. All this can be told in simple, ordinary language, and if it's properly dramatized and made interesting, it will go a long way toward explaining the *meaning* of this scientific development: not exactly what was done, but why and how it was done. It will give the layman an explanation he can understand, and usually that will be all he wants.

There is, of course, a third kind of explanation, a mathematical explanation of the machine for mathematicians. This, too, can be put in simple language, that is, short sentences, simple words and so on, and that will save mathematicians time and effort in reading their professional journals. But—let's face it—the layman will never understand the formulas and graphs. To understand exactly what Commander Aiken has done, you have to have so-and-so many years of higher mathematics, and that's that.

Or let's take another example that happens to be handy. How can the scientific yardstick formula of this book be explained? The answer is exactly the same. Again, there are three levels of explanation, two for laymen, one for scientists only. First, there is the *operation* of the formula: that can be explained by the simple set of directions which you will find in the back of the book. Second, there is the *meaning* of the formula: to explain that properly, I would have to go into the history of language simplifying, the relationship between language and understanding, the readability formulas that were developed by other researchers, the differences between those formulas and this one, and so on. Then I could dramatize the whole story and that would probably give most people all the explanation they want. However, there is still the third level, that of the *scientific* explanation; and here I would have to get into statistical regression formulas and multiple correlation and whatnot, and nobody who hasn't had a course in statistics would know what I am talking about.

Now let's see how the principles of language simplifying apply to these three types of scientific explanation. First, let's take a look at the language of operation sheets, directions, shop manuals, popular mechanics, the literature that tells how to do a technical job. Here is an example I picked at random from a book on papermaking:

> In the event of there being more than one screen serving the machine (as is usually the case) it is necessary to watch carefully the operation of the screens with reference to the stock supplied them, and each valve should be opened or closed in proportion to the capacity of the screen it is feeding. If there is any difference in the capacities of the screens, it is probably due to the cams or toe-blocks being worn, or some other thing affecting the oscillation of the diaphragm.

Now obviously this is not very readable. But what are the obstacles the reader has to face? Certainly *not* the technical terms; in fact, any reader interested in papermaking machines is apt to know what a cam or a toe-block is, and if not, will have no trouble finding out. But that technical knowledge won't make it any easier for him to work his way through "in the event of there being" or "with reference to the stock supplied them" or "in proportion to the capacity." The simple fact is that people who know something about certain technical operations are usually those least equipped for writing about them or explaining what they know to somebody else.

Not so long ago a *New York Times* story described the excellent instruction manuals put out by Bell Telephone Laboratories for the Army and Navy. Let me quote one sentence: "The company has discovered that it is easier to hire a qualified editor and teach him what he needs to know about

the technical terms involved than it would be to take a quali
fied engineer and teach him what he would need to know
about the art of editing . . ."

If those papermakers had followed the same principle, our
passage would probably read somewhat like this:

> Usually the machine is served by more than one screen
> If so, watch carefully how much stock goes through each
> To keep the flow even, just open or close the valves. (If
> you want to make the screens work evenly, look first for
> worn cams or toe-blocks. Most often that's what makes the
> difference.)

In other words, all writing of the operation-sheet type
should address the reader directly, and should tell him step
by step what to do. It's as simple as that. Anybody who writes
how-to-do prose should start off by reading a good cookbook;
here, for instance, is a model paragraph from Fannie Farmer:

> Apple Pie
>
> Line pie plate with pastry. Pare, core, and cut apples
> in eighths, put row around plate ½ inch from edge, and
> work towards center until plate is covered; then pile on
> remainder. Mix sugar, nutmeg, salt, lemon juice, and
> grated rind, and sprinkle over apples. Dot over with
> butter. Wet edges of undercrust, cover with upper crust
> and press edges together. Prick several places with fork
> Bake.

Anybody can understand that, and anybody can understand
any kind of technical directions that are written in the same
style.

When we come to the second level of scientific explanation
we find, oddly enough, that there is also one single standard
formula. The reason is simple: Since the meaning of any mod
ern scientific fact can only be explained by the method of it
discovery, and since the scientific method is the same in all
branches of science, any such explanation will be the story of
a scientist, or several scientists, going through the classic four
stages of modern scientific method: observation, hypothesis

deduction, and experimental verification. So this type of popularization will show how a scientist got curious about certain facts, thought up a theory to explain them, devised experiments to prove the theory, and finally tested it and found that it worked. If two scientists working on the same problem can be shown, so much the better: this will make the reader appreciate not only the scientific method, but also the fact that modern science is never a one-man affair.

Popular science written by this standard formula is probably the most educational type of writing there is: it's the only way of making laymen appreciate scientific method. But let's not get into this; let me rather show you a classic example. This is from a *Reader's Digest* article on penicillin by J. D. Ratcliff:

> The story of penicillin begins in 1929, when Dr. Alexander Fleming . . . was examining a glass culture plate milky with millions of bacteria. His sharp eye detected something. There was a fleck of green mold on the plate, and around this fleck was a halo of clear fluid. *Something was destroying the bacteria!* A mold that had dropped in from the air was causing their sudden death on an unprecedented scale . . .
>
> Dr. Fleming fished out the mold but research on it stood still for ten years . . . Then the sulfa drugs came along to reawaken interest in this field.
>
> The sulfa drugs were amazing performers against some bacterial diseases; sorry failures against others. Something better was needed . . . Dr. Howard Florey of Oxford remembered Fleming's work. That green mold was poison to bacteria on culture plates. Might it not also work in the bodies of men?
>
> Florey and his colleagues . . . decided to investigate . . . They set to work at the tedious task of growing the green mold in earthen-ware flasks. When the mold had grown into a hard, rubbery mat the chemists took over. Hidden somewhere in the mold was a bacteria killer.
>
> By a slow process of elimination, the chemists discarded

> chemical components of the mold that had no antibacterial effect. In the end they turned up with the minutest pinch of a yellow-brown powdery stuff. This *might* be the bacteria murderer.
>
> The first trials of the yellow powder were run in test tubes. It appeared that as little as one part in 160 million would slow the growth of bacteria! . . . This looked splendid. But there was still a big hurdle to overcome. The stuff somehow poisoned microbes. Might it not also poison men?
>
> Florey and his helpers . . . shot huge doses of sure streptococcus death into 50 mice. Then the mice were divided into two groups of 25 each. One group would get no further attention; the other would get penicillin.
>
> Within 17 hours all the unprotected mice were dead . . . Hundreds of other mice trials followed, with similarly favorable results.
>
> At last Florey was ready to carry his work from mice to men . . .

And so on. This is science for laymen at its best, and it's written in typical *Reader's Digest* manner, so that an average person can understand it. But I hope you realize that it is a piece of what might be called science appreciation, not of scientific explanation. It does not even have the chemical formula for penicillin in it. In short, from a scientist's point of view, it offers no explanation at all.

To explain science fully, as I said before, you will have to use a third level of explanation, and this is where the layman will never be able to keep up with you. Suppose, for instance, you are asked for an explanation of what retene is, and the Encyclopædia Britannica gives you the following clue:

> RETENE, an aromatic hydrocarbon occurring in wood tars and obtained by distilling resinous woods. It crystallises in colourless plates melting at 98.5° C and boiling at 394° C. Chronic acid oxidises the hydrocarbon to retene quinone (an *ortho*diketone) and permanganate oxidises the quinon to 3-hydroxy-*iso*propyldiphenyl—1:1′:2′—tri

carboxylic acid. These reactions show that retene is thyl*iso*propylphenanthrene, $C_{18}H_{18}$, with the adjacent structural formula.

Plainly, there is no way of really telling a layman what retene is. To understand it, with or without simple language, you have to be a chemist, and that's that.

There is only one bit of advice I can offer in this business of giving laymen an exact scientific explanation: don't try. It is far better to be as frank as Bertrand Russell in his popular explanation of the relativity theory, who says at one point:

> . . . this part can be expressed by the method of "tensors." The importance of this method can hardly be exaggerated; it is, however, quite impossible to explain it in non-mathematical terms.

Or, if you are unfortunate enough to be assigned to such an impossible job, you might add some sort of apology, the way Gove Hambidge did in the 1941 Yearbook of Agriculture:

> . . . The editor would like to point out that to visualize even the more elementary aspects of atmospheric circulation over the earth is not easy, since you have to imagine that you are a mile or two up in the air, on your stomach with your head toward the North Pole, a clock nearby lying on its back so you can readily tell which is clockwise and which counter-clockwise rotation—also a mirror so you can see how everything would be reversed if you were in the Southern instead of the Northern Hemisphere, and you have to remember constantly that a south wind is a northward-moving wind, an east wind a westward-moving wind, and vice versa.

Chapter XVII

THE TROUBLE WITH TEXTBOOKS

THERE are some things, as I said, that can never be ex plained to laymen; but that doesn't mean that they canno be explained at all. If a layman cannot understand them, the he must try to stop being a layman: in other words, he mus study up to the point where he can keep up with the expert explanations. The simplest way to do this is to go to a librar and take out a textbook.

But this is where the trouble starts. You sit down with textbook, you open it, and after a short while you discover yo can't read it. For some reason, *it just doesn't read.* It's to textbooky, too dry, too dull—you can't put your finger on i but there is some invisible obstacle, and you don't seem t get anywhere.

Don't get discouraged. Everybody knows that textbooks a unreadable, even educators. Here is what a committee of tl American Council on Education had to say about them r cently: "An ordinary textbook is a compact body of factu statements which does not invite or permit fluent reading

Why is this so? The main reason is simple: textboo are written for teachers, not for students. The textbook writ is the only writer in the world who doesn't have to wor about his readers: as long as his book pleases the teache it will be "required reading," that is, students will be forc to read it whether they like it or not. So, naturally, the te book writer doesn't care a bit whether his book will be pleasa to read or interesting or well written; he knows that tl isn't what teachers care about most. Teachers look first f other things in a textbook: whether it is well organized f teaching, whether it has good exercises, whether it has a lot of information—in other words, whether it will be a help in teaching, a laborsaving device. As a result, textbooks are what they are. In case you have forgotten since school days, here is a batch of quotes from a typical example (a widely used high-school text in American history):

> Transportation and communication had not been developed sufficiently to bring the people together, and since they lived far apart and since the different sections of the country had different economic interests resulting from different physical conditions which tended to make for sectionalism, it was difficult to secure national unity . . .
>
> The spirit of nationalism began to take definite form in the minds of many of the Republicans as they attacked some of the practical problems of government . . .
>
> The blessings of independence were tempered with certain disadvantages . . .
>
> Slavery, on the whole, was characterized by many objectionable features . . .
>
> Great as were the economic and social problems, they were soon overshadowed by, and to a great extent merged into, the political problem . . .
>
> Another important problem which has commanded attention throughout our entire history is that of money . . .
>
> Money, which is so important in our industrial life today, has played an important part throughout our entire history . . .
>
> With the recent deplorable condition of farmers in mind, let us look at the history of the American farmer . . .
>
> Perhaps the most striking difference between a locomotive in use today and that of a century ago is in the size. *The Best Friend* or the *York* would be a pygmy indeed in comparison with one of the great compound locomotives now in use on some of our roads . . .
>
> Few, if any, of the problems of our early railroad companies were more pressing than the financial . . .

> Inasmuch as the earliest methods of communication in America were by direct speech or by written messages, improvements in communication very naturally depended upon the progress in transportation . . .
>
> The first half of the nineteenth century was characterized by a religious enthusiasm which evidenced itself in revivals and camp meetings and in humanitarian reform . . .
>
> The shorter working day made available more time for leisure, and the nervous strain caused by our complex social and economic system with its keen competition not only made recreation desirable but made occasional relaxation necessary . . .

Now can you imagine a high-school boy or girl reading this with the slightest interest? Can you imagine anybody, for that matter, struggling through all these "important problems," "characteristic features," and "certain disadvantages," through the "inasmuchs," "perhapses" and "to-a-great-extents"—and learn and remember something about American history? Mind you, this is a good textbook, as textbooks go, in one of the most interesting of all subjects; there are many, many thousands that are worse.

There is no secret about how to write a good textbook. The most important rule is to write for the student and not for the teacher; everything else follows.

Naturally, our yardstick formula can be used to key the style of the book to the grade where it is to be used (see the table on page 135); but that's only a beginning. Aside from being easy to read, the book must also be a help in studying; after all, the reader is entitled to get an expertly designed learning tool for his money. This means that a good textbook should be built upon modern psychological principles so that the reader gets the most out of it; it should be a machine to make things understood, remembered, and applied. Just how to do this has been described recently in an article by Professor Thomas H. Briggs in *School and Society*. Professor Briggs knows what he is talking about. Here are some of his recommendations:

> Make the purpose of each unit clear to the pupils and of such importance that, appreciating its value, they will accept it as their own . . .
>
> A good textbook should help to increase the pupil's power to retain and to use . . . It should constantly help pupils to discriminate between facts that must be learned and permanently retained and those that are for the purpose of clarification and support of the essential . . .
>
> A text may well give some directions as to how to profit most from a lecture . . .
>
> The style of writing should be simple and absolutely clear on a first reading . . . Vocabulary often receives the chief blame for reading difficulties, but . . . sentences cause more difficulties than single words . . .
>
> Do not be afraid to repeat an idea in other words, to elaborate it and to give illustrations, both verbal and pictorial. This will result in longer texts than are commonly used in schools. As a rule the shortest books are the hardest to read . . .
>
> A good pattern for the authors in each unit is (a) to state what they are going to say; (b) to say it simply and completely; (c) to tell in a summary that makes the relations clear what they have said . . .
>
> A style is usually more interesting if it contains personal anecdotes. Use freely the names and incidents of people . . .

I know at least one book that seems to be written strictly according to Briggs, only more so. It doesn't really come under the heading of textbook, and it's unacademic; but many people must have liked it and thought they got something out of it, since it sold several million copies. I mean *How to Win Friends and Influence People* by Dale Carnegie.

Here are a few applications of Professor Briggs's points from Carnegie's book. For instance, Professor Briggs recommends stressing important points; this is how Carnegie does it:

> ...If you are inclined to tell people they are wrong, please read the following paragraph on your knees every morning before breakfast...

Or, Professor Briggs thinks a textbook should include directions as to how to profit most from a lecture. Carnegie goes beyond that; he has five pages with "Nine Suggestions on How to Get the Most Out of This Book."

Or, Professor Briggs recommends a simple style. Carnegie is 100 per cent conversational, to the point of repeating words and phrases—like this, for instance:

> "Mrs. Lincoln's loud, shrill voice," wrote the late Senator Albert J. Beveridge, the most distinguished Lincoln authority of this generation—"Mrs. Lincoln's loud, shrill voice could be heard across the street . . . "

Or, Professor Briggs suggests repetition "in other words." Carnegie doesn't hesitate to repeat *the same words* if he thinks it necessary:

> The Chinese have a proverb pregnant with the age-old wisdom of the changeless East: "He who treads softly goes far."
>
> They have spent five thousand years studying human nature, those cultured Chinese, and they have garnered a lot of perspicacity: "He who treads softly goes far."

Professor Briggs thinks a textbook author should in each unit tell what he is going to tell, tell it, and tell what he has told. Carnegie uses this technique not only for each chapter but for each section, and for the book as a whole.

Professor Briggs believes in the free use of personal anecdotes. Carnegie uses practically nothing but anecdotes to make hi points.

And so on. In short, anyone who is about to write a textbook would do well to spend an evening reading *How to Wi Friends and Influence People,* strictly as an example of *how t teach in print.*

As a substitute for textbook writers who are too highbro

to touch an all-time best seller with a ten-foot pole, I recommend *America* by Stephen Vincent Benét. The late poet wrote this textbook on American history, shortly before his death, as an assignment for the Office of War Information, to be translated and used abroad. He, too, used simple English and the tricks recommended by Professor Briggs. Here is how he tells about the Pilgrims:

> The Pilgrims landed on November 11, 1620, from a ship called the *Mayflower*.
>
> Who were the Pilgrims and why did they come to America? Were they adventurers, conquerors, gold seekers?
>
> No, they were not. A few of those on the *Mayflower* came on the chance of getting land and farms of their own. But most came for another reason. They came because they wished to worship God in their own way—a simple and faithful way, but not the way of the Established Church of the England of their time.
>
> They were family men, for the most part. They brought their wives and their children with them on a 64-day voyage, in a small tossing ship. One child was born on the voyage, two others just after the landfall. The whole company numbered a little over a hundred human beings. It was backed by an English company whose investors put money into the venture. But the backbone of the venture was this group of quiet, family men, bringing their wives and children to a coast at the world's end.
>
> Why did they do such a crazy thing? Why on earth did they take such a chance? Nobody ordered them to do it, bribed them to do it. They went to great trouble and pain, uprooted their homes, left everything they had known behind, from the memories of childhood to the things in the house that one looks at and cannot take because there will be no room, and yet remembers.
>
> They wanted to worship God in their own way. They were resolved and determined to worship God in their own way . . .

I suppose you will be curious to know how this topic is treated in the high-school textbook I quoted earlier in this chapter. Here it is:

> The first permanent settlement in New England was made by the Pilgrims, or Separatists, who established a colony on the coast of Massachusetts in 1620. This settlement, like Jamestown, was promoted by a commercial company. These early settlers were interested in improving their economic condition, but there was another factor which played a very important part, namely, religion...

And that's about all that needs to be said about the writing of textbooks—except for one thing. Textbooks, as I said, don't depend upon acceptance by their readers; they are not written by people who make a living by writing; they are usually done in a hurry and on the side; and all that means that the things you are apt to find in a typical textbook are usually trite, often wrong, and sometimes downright nonsense. This book is not the place to go into that side of textbook writing, but I think, just for the fun of it, we might take a few minutes to look over a textbook on rhetoric and composition—the subject of this book. This is what college students are taught these days:

> Subordination of clauses:
>
> Weak: Yesterday I was sitting in my front yard when a car crashed through the hedge.
>
> Proper subordination: Yesterday, when I was sitting in my yard, a car crashed through the hedge.

(The so-called weak sentence is good, conversational English; the "proper subordination" completely spoils the surprise.)

> A writer can nearly always strengthen the force of an expression that seems to him somewhat feeble by changing the more important loose sentences into the periodic form...
>
> Loose: My poor grades were the subject of the dean's talk to me, after he had asked about my father's

health and how soon the new fraternity house would be completed.

Periodic: The subject of the dean's talk to me, after he had asked about my father's health and how soon the new fraernity house would be completed, was my poor grades.

(Both sentences are very feeble, but the recommended periodic sentence is clearly feebler. Nobody talks like that, anyway.)

In conversation, rhetorical questions and exclamations are naturally quite often resorted to. In order to stress certain of our remarks, we ask: "What was to be done next?" Or we exclaim in some such fashion as this: "Would that I could call back what I said next!" In writing, except of a very informal nature, rhetorical devices of this kind should seldom, if ever, be used for the purpose of securing emphasis.

(So rhetorical devices are too informal for good writing, is that it? And are these maiden-auntish examples of conversation supposed to be taken from real life?)

Yes, I realize that the trouble with textbooks is not just the style. Maybe it's a blessing that most of them do not "invite or permit fluent reading."

Chapter XVIII

WHAT PRICE COPY?

AMONG writers, there is one group who really have gone to town with psychology and modern research methods: I mean, of course, the advertising copy writers. Only this one among all the branches of writing can boast of a whole shelf of scientific handbooks on how to write, of costly readership investigations, of experimental tests of words and word combinations. The copy writers have it all figured out. The result? Simplicity is best. "Simple advertising costs least and sells most," says Kenneth M. Goode in his book *How to Write Advertising*, and literally every book on the subject repeats this advice in more or less the same words. It's an established fact that

DRINK COCA-COLA

or

CALL FOR PHILIP MORRIS

are just about the best ads there are.

So far, so good; and there wouldn't be any point in mentioning advertising in a book on plain talk if all copy writers would follow that simple pattern. But they don't; and a typical ad reads like this:

(Picture of a woman and two children reading a letter)

"MY DEAREST THREE . . ."

A gentle young wife. Two tousle-headed kiddies. This Dresden-china trio is the dynamo that powers the toughest marine in the outfit.

Don't let *your* fighting man down; don't relax *your* war efforts. Our heartening victories do not mean that shortages are over. Textiles, for instance—particularly sheets—will continue to be scarce. So coax every last bit of wear out of the sheets you have, and when at last it becomes necessary to replace them, buy wisely.

Look for the best possible combination of desired qualities at the lowest price. Look for *Pacific* Sheets, in which smoothness, softness, whiteness, firmness and strength are skilfully *balanced* to give you the utmost in service and comfort . . .

Or here is another typical ad:

(Picture of a baby)

Y'KNOW, I'M NEW HERE . . .

Indeed you are! And I'm afraid you'll find things are different today than if you'd arrived a few years ago.

"Different?" How do you mean?

Take telephones, as an example. Before the war, we were glad to install one for everybody who asked. Now there are few available, and folks must wait their turn . . . because manpower and manufacturing facilities are needed to make communications and electronic equipment for our fighting men . . .

Here is a third one:

(Picture of George Washington in a jeep)

GEORGE WASHINGTON COULD HAVE HAD A JEEP

All the raw materials needed to build a jeep were obtainable in George Washington's time.

Only the knowledge of how to obtain them, refine them and fabricate them into such a vehicle was lacking.

At Alcoa, we call this important ingredient "Imagineering." That's our handy word for letting imagination soar and then engineering it down to practical use . . .

You see what all these ads have in common? You have noticed, of course, that they are written in the same unmistakable advertising jargon. But why is that? Well, let's look at the situation: Here is the reader happily enjoying a piece of interesting news in *Time* or a pleasantly sentimental story in *Good Housekeeping*. It's the copy writer's job to interrupt the reader with something so startling or engaging that he or she will switch from the story to the ad. Then, once the reader is caught by the ad headline—the baby, the mother and children, Washington in a jeep—there follows some tricky word juggling and all of a sudden he or she is reading about sheets, or telephones, or aluminum. The rest is easy: with the help of a phony "for instance" or an arrogant "at" the name of the client is slipped in; a few expensive-looking touches are added (a Dresden-china dynamo or "imagineering"); and there we are.

In fact, this sort of ad practically writes itself. Here is a cigarette ad with a Hamlet theme:

> (Picture of Hamlet, in black, with Yorick's skull, smoking a cigarette)
>
> IF HAMLET HAD KNOWN CIGARETTES
>
> he would never have thought of suicide. He would have soothed his nerves with the richly energizing mellowness . . . the full-spirited aroma . . . the inspiring, top-of-the-world flavor of modern tobacco products.
>
> At Stinkweeds, we call this vital something "enthusability.". . .

And so on. You can write this kind of ad for yourself. Or you can learn about "livability" in Du Pont's poultry feed ads, about "see-ability" in Westinghouse ads for Mazda lamps, about "soloing" in Weil's perfume ads (". . . and the woman who wears COBRA stands out alone in all her beauty like some divine instrument soloing to the gods"), or about any other imaginable word a copy writer could think up.

The fact is that copy writing has got into a rut. They have

their psychological rules, and their readership tests, and their refined copy-research methods, but with all that they got themselves deeper and deeper into the catch-phrase and word-magic business. In short, most advertising copy nowadays is being written to satisfy the seller rather than the buyer.

Otherwise, copy writers would naturally think about what their readers are doing, what mood they are in, what kind of writing they will welcome. They would not try to play tricks on the reader, to bamboozle him out of what he is reading into reading something entirely different, to hammer brand names into his unwilling mind. Instead, they would carefully analyze what the reader is apt to find on the same magazine or newspaper page, or the kind of entertainment he is getting in the sponsored radio program. Then, knowing exactly the characteristics of the context, they would prepare the copy so that it fits in most naturally and casually. And that kind of copy would sell.

Obviously, such copy fitting could be done by using our yardstick formula and the other techniques of language analysis described in this book. But there are a few rare copy writers who can do this kind of thing by feel or whatever you want to call it. This gives me a chance to show you a few examples of what I am talking about:

First, an ad in the *New Yorker*, written in the profile manner:

(Cartoon of Mr. Bambucci)

THIS IS OUR MR. BAMBUCCI

For all we know, Mr. Bambucci may be the only ladies' tailor in New York who celebrates February's Mardi Gras season by killing a pig. This is a spirited custom he brought over from Italy 21 years ago, when he came to this country as a tailor's apprentice, and wound up working for Saks Fifth Avenue.

As for what happens to the pig, first Mr. Bambucci grooms it to a T., on his farm upstate. Come February, he kills it. Then, in true carnival tradition, he invites all his friends . . .

Next, a *Ladies' Home Journal* ad in the slick-paper story manner:

(Picture of a girl)

I'M LOOKING FOR A SERGEANT IN AN UNIRONED SHIRT . . .

. . . And for a better way of living after the war.

It's the way we planned in a two-by-four tourist cabin one night, sitting on a suit-case in the middle of the floor. Sounds crazy? Maybe, but you do crazy things in war-time. . . . Here's the story:

It happened on my last week-end at Ken's camp. As usual, he'd staggered in with BAGS of dirty laundry. And as usual, I'd gone into my "little-woman" act and dumped 'em all in the bathtub.

Then came the sudden change in orders—*"All passes canceled. Report back at midnight."* We looked at those wet shirts hung on the shower-rod . . . and then at each other. *"Holy cow."* said Ken, sort of blankly . . .

And here is a *Time* ad, written in perfect *Time*style:

EYESIGHT

Television Vision

No great commercial shakes before Pearl Harbor, television is now postwar dream product "most likely to succeed." Televisionaries scatter some exciting hints of things to come:

¶ Medical students will witness surgical operations performed in distant hospitals.

¶ People will see and hear Congress in action, thus more accurately appraise men in public life.

¶ By 1950, national networks will carry live entertainment, sporting events, spot news into 25 million U. S. homes.

Still unsettled: the heated question whether television will utilize present 525-line screen or newly-developed

1000-line screen. Latter gives sharper, better detailed telimages, requires scrapping of all present telequipment—a costly loss. . . .

As I said, such examples of perfect copy-fitting are rare. Ordinarily, you couldn't possibly guess from the style of an ad where it appeared. Want to try? All right, here goes:

> . . . a potentially troublesome group of bacteria, known as the Secondary Invaders, can take advantage of a below-par condition and stage a "mass invasion" of the mucous membrane to produce many of a cold's complications and much of its misery.
>
> Our own research results seem to indicate that the repeated use of Listerine Antiseptic, by killing huge numbers of these secondary invaders, helps nature to halt many a "mass invasion" and the resultant misery of infection.
>
> Over and over again test data has confirmed the ability of Listerine Antiseptic to accomplish bacterial reductions on mouth and throat surfaces ranging up to 96.7% fifteen minutes after a gargle; up to 80% an hour after.
>
> Even more impressive is the data resulting from clinical tests conducted over a period of twelve years . . .

Now guess where this ad was printed. In the *Dentists' Journal*? Wrong. In *Popular Science*? Wrong again. It appeared in the *Ladies' Home Journal*.

And where do you think this comes from?

> . . . You can spell the future of America after the war—and that of every American—in just four letters: JOBS.
>
> *Jobs!* Not relief checks. Not charity. Not the handouts of a grateful government . . . but the kind of jobs that America has stood for these 169 years.
>
> To build jobs like these for all those willing and desperately anxious to work at them means *keeping America's factories running*. It means pouring out goods for *peace*—at close to the rate at which goods are now being poured out for war . . .

You would guess that this bit of rather primitive economics is meant for mass consumption, wouldn't you? Sounds like stuff for pulp magazine readers, doesn't it—with a touch of talking down? Sorry, you're wrong again: it's from an advertising message to executives in the *New York Times.*

Of course, it may not always be possible to write copy that fits exactly the medium. Sometimes the writer does not know where the ad will appear, sometimes there is only one type of copy for widely different media. The thing to do in such a case is to be as simple, clear, and to the point as possible. A sincere explanation of what one has to sell and why it is worth having will be good copy anywhere. It may lack sophistication, and the competitors may laugh at its simple appeal, but it will do the work.

Here, for instance, is an ad that will make most highbrows wince (E. B. White wrote an excellent satirical poem about it in the *New Yorker*):

> Walter J. Black, President of the Classics Club,
> invites you to accept free
> This Beautifully Bound, Superbly Decorated Edition of
>
> PLATO
> FIVE GREAT DIALOGUES
>
> It is amazing how this great classic—written over 2,000 years ago—hits so many nails squarely on the head today. Here is how to look at love, learning, friendship . . . how to live an intelligently *happy* life. . . . In these conversations between friends—fresh, humorous, informal—you have the book on which so much of man's thinking has been founded . . .
>
> Why Are Great Books Called "Classics"?
>
> A true "classic" is a living book that will never grow old. For sheer fascination it can rival the most thrilling modern novel. Perhaps you have often wondered how these truly great books, "got that way." First, because they are so readable. They would not have lived unless they were read, and they would not have been read unless

> they were interesting. And to be interesting they had to be easy to understand. Those are the very qualities which characterize these selections: *readability, interest, simplicity.*

Now that's not a perfect ad. It has its mannerisms, and it's written in not very good English. But if you think what it means to talk people who never had the advantages of a college education into buying Plato, Erasmus and whatnot at $1.39 apiece, you will realize how well this ad does its job. It explains clearly and accurately what's in Plato's *Dialogues,* and why anybody should spend money on such a book. Then it goes on to explain, again quite naturally, what makes a classic a classic and how wrong it is to be scared of reading them. And so on. There is not a word in the ad that would not fit the mind or the mood of anybody who might become a member of the Classics Club.

Time, not so long ago, told the success story of another simple ad. It seems that the two owners of the Londonderry Ice Cream Company "spent $30,000 in three years running big, lush color ads in newspapers—all with 'uniformly lousy results.' The trouble was . . . that these ads plugged the name Londonderry instead of telling people how they could make ice cream cheaper at home than they could buy it." Success came when Londonderry switched to the following simple ad:

> Ice Cream. As low as 8¢ a pint. Sure to be pure—you make it. Combine cream, milk or evaporated milk, sugar and Londonderry. Whip—then freeze—that's all. No ice crystals . . . 15¢ package makes 2 qts., any flavor.

Here you have the perfect ad: clear, easy to read, and it sells ice cream. Next time you are tempted by imagineering or something, remember this ad. It will do you good:

> Ice Cream. As low as 8¢ a pint. Sure to be pure—you make it. Combine cream, milk or evaporated milk, sugar and Londonderry. Whip—then freeze—that's all. No ice crystals . . . 15¢ package makes 2 qts., any flavor.

Chapter XIX

HOW TO READ THE FEDERAL REGISTER

SUPPOSE you take an issue of the Federal Register (where all executive orders are printed), open it at random and read this:

> Upon consideration of a plan for joint action filed with the Office of Defense Transportation by the persons named in Appendix 1 hereof to facilitate compliance with the requirements and purposes of General Order ODT 3 Revised, as amended (7 F.R. 5445, 6689, 7694; 8 F.R. 4660, 14582; 9 F.R. 2793, 3264, 3357, 6778), a copy of which plan is attached hereto as Appendix 2, and
>
> It appearing that the proposed coordination of operations is necessary in order to assure maximum utilization of the facilities, services, and equipment, and to conserve and providently utilize, vital equipment, materials, and supplies, of the carriers, and to provide for the prompt and continuous movement of necessary traffic, the attainment of which purposes is essential to the successful prosecution of the war;
>
> *It is hereby ordered,* That:
>
> 1. The plan for joint action above referred to is hereby approved and the carriers are directed to put the plan in operation forthwith, subject to the following provisions, which shall supersede any provisions of such plan that are in conflict therewith . . .

And so on, point 2 to point 9, for two more columns. Now what is all this? What does it mean, if anything? How is anyone supposed to read it and make sense out of it?

If we analyze Federal Register prose with our yardstick formula, we find that it is obviously designed to make reading as difficult as possible. The sentences simply never stop, colloquial root words are carefully avoided, and there is never a hint of who is talking to whom. On top of that, just to make sure nobody can read straight through, paragraphs are tied together with *ands* and *thats,* fancy legalisms like *hereto* or *therewith* litter each line, and names that *have* to be mentioned are skilfully tucked away in the appendix.

As we stare at our random issue of the Federal Register and wonder why the government tries so hard to make its publications unreadable, we suddenly find a clue to the puzzle. After the nine-point ODT co-ordination order with which we started, there follows another nine-point ODT co-ordination order *in exactly the same words* (only the persons mentioned in Appendix 1 are different). This is startling; but as we look further, we find a third identical order—and a fourth—and a fifth. In fact, the whole issue seems to be full of repetitions of one and the same order. As we count up, we find that there are *seventeen* of them, all starting with "Upon consideration . . ." and winding up with the appendix.

Slowly we begin to understand. The Federal Register is not supposed to be read at all. It simply prints things so that someday, somewhere, some government official can say: "Yes, but it says in the Federal Register . . ." All this government stuff, in other words, is not reading matter, but prefabricated parts of quarrels.

If nobody would ever quarrel with us, the government says, we could write such a co-ordination order very simply:

Fast Freight Lines Inc.
and
Trustworthy Trucking Company

Gentlemen:

You recently filed with us a plan for joint action. We approve of it and you can start right away. Follow these rules: . . .

And so on. But, the government says, somebody will say we had no right to issue such an order; so let's put in something about "essential to the successful prosecution of the war." And then somebody will say that the original General Order was never published; so let's give the page numbers in the Federal Register right here. And then somebody will say that his case is different from that of the 16 other companies; so let's print the order 17 times over, once for each company. And somebody will say this and somebody will say that; and people will try to tear sentences out of context, so let's work everything into one sentence; they will deliberately read false references into pronouns, so let's never use pronouns but repeat *such plan* each time we talk about it; they will say that *requirements* doesn't mean *purposes*, so let's write "requirements and purposes"; they will say that *conserve* is not the same as *utilize*, so let's put in "conserve and utilize"; then they will say *utilize* means to use in any old way, so let's make it "conserve and providently utilize" . . . In short, the government says, citizens are mean, quarrelsome characters who will break every rule at the drop of a comma; so let's be just as nasty from the start and block every possible move with a blistering, armed-to-the-teeth order.

So, if you, a peaceful, law-abiding citizen, want to read something that is written in Federalese, here is what you do:

First, try by all means to find a rewrite, press release, covering letter, or anything where the same information is given without all the quarrelsome byplay. Only if there is nothing else, read the original.

Second, skip everything that is just a formal requirement and try to find the meat as quickly as possible. Don't turn back to read the preamble; it isn't worth it.

Third, find out who is covered. (In our sample ODT order you would start with the tail end, Appendix 1, and find, in small print, that this order deals with Fast Freight Lines, Inc and The Trustworthy Trucking Company.)

Fourth, don't bother about finding out who wrote the stuff Government officials are famous for never signing what they write and never reading what they sign. (Our sample ODT order is signed by the ODT Administrator, who never read it, and was written by a subordinate official whose name you'll never know.) That's why Federalese is full of *it's* and passive constructions. "It is hereby ordered" is the typical buck-passing sentence: try to find out who is ordering you around, and they'll send you up and down the line.

Fifth, remember that an ordinary case like yours doesn't interest the government which is busy fending off all those inveterate lawbreakers. You are barely mentioned between the lines, if at all. Here, for instance, is a sentence from a price regulation:

> Unless . . .

(Naturally, since most government orders deal with unlikely possibilities somebody might bring up, the most popular word in Federalese is *unless*. It so happens that *unless* is also the most difficult word in the English language. Try to read and understand "Unless you don't disapprove of saying no, you won't refuse.") Here we go again:

> Unless the Office of Price Administration or an authorized representative thereof shall, by letter mailed to the applicant within 21 days from the date of filing the application, disapprove the maximum price as reported, such price shall be deemed to have been approved, subject to non-retroactive written disapproval or adjustment at any later time by the Office of Price Administration.

Now what does that mean for an ordinary person who has eported a ceiling price? Let's see: Suppose your price is not o high that OPA would disapprove of it. Then OPA would imply not answer and if 21 days go by without an answer, ou would know that your ceiling is all right. All you have to lo is to send in your application and sit tight for three weeks. o here is what the Federal Register says between the lines:

> You must wait three weeks before you can charge the ceiling price you applied for. OPA can always change that price. If they do, they will write you a letter.

Sixth, whenever the government says something in a negative form, turn it around to see what it means. For example:

> Sale at wholesale means a sale of corn in less than carload quantity by a person other than one acting in the capacity of a producer or country shipper to (1) any person, other than a feeder; or (2) a feeder in quantities of 30,000 pounds or more.

Now suppose you rewrite this without a single *other than* like this:

> Sales at wholesale are sales of less than a carload of corn by anyone except producers and country shippers. However, sales of less than 30,000 pounds to feeders are sales at retail.

Rather simple, isn't it?

Seventh . . . But now I am running out of simple rules. Or, rather, I am running out of special rules for Federalese. After all, underneath the particular features of the nasty, or official, style, there are all the stock elements of bad and unreadable style, and you are back in the familiar game of breaking up worm-sentences, substituting *help* for *facilitate*, writing *you* instead of "the persons named in Appendix 1," making "upon consideration" into "we have considered," hunting for *whiches* that should be *thats* and so on and so on. The only difference is that officialese is, on the average, worse than any other kind of writing, so that rewriting it in everyday English seems often almost impossible.

So, when we get down to it, the answer to the question how to read the Federal Register is the same as to the question how to read any other difficult writing: translate it into your own words, as you would use them in conversation. That's a big order, I know, but it's often the only possible way to read and understand Uncle Sam's own prose. Here he is talking about fish, for instance:

> The maximum price for a primary fish shipper sale of fresh fish or seafood (except shrimp, salmon or halibut

to a retailer or purveyor of meals where the sale is negotiated or made at a branch warehouse as herein defined and where the fish or seafood is sold and delivered from the stock of a primary fish shipper wholesaler's branch warehouse which is remote from his main place of doing business, and at which warehouse the primary fish shipper employs two or more full-time employees who are stationed at and engaged in making sales and performing services solely for the primary fish shipper from such warehouse is the price listed in Table D in §22 plus the allowance provided in §6 for a service and delivery sale where such a sale is made, plus the transportation allowance in §9, plus the appropriate container allowance in §21.

Now, if you had to explain this business to someone, you would mention a primary fish shipper—whatever that is—only once instead of four times (that's what pronouns have been invented for); you would talk about the exception for shrimps whenever you get to talking about shrimps but not before; you would add your explanation of what you mean by a branch warehouse at the end, just in case; you would call an eating place an eating place and not a purveyor of meals; you wouldn't talk about employing employees; and you wouldn't bother with paragraph numbers nobody can remember anyway. You would say something like this:

> If you are a primary fish shipper and sell to retailers or eating places from a branch warehouse, find your ceiling prices in Table D. You can charge extra for containers, freight, service and delivery. (Branch warehouse means a warehouse far from your main office, where at least two people work for you full time.)

Let's try another one, about rutabaga and stuff:

> The maximum prices for the sale or delivery of the varieties of beet, carrot, onion, rutabaga, and turnip seeds which are specified in a memorandum from E. J. Murphy, Chief, Grain Products Branch of the Food Dis-

> tribution Administration to Commercial Vegetable Seed Growers, and dated October 30, 1943, by a farmer-producer (except as provided in subparagraph (2) and (3) hereof) shall be the prices as specified in said memorandum on or prior to the date of the issuance of this regulation which commercial seed growers are required to pay farmer seed growers per pound for such varieties of vegetable seeds in order to be eligible to sell or deliver the same to the Federal Surplus Commodities Corporation, plus transportation charges from the farm where grown to the buyer's receiving point by a usual route and method of transportation.

What's this about? Someone called Murphy wrote a memorandum with a list of prices, and these prices are now made ceiling prices. Again, let's leave the subparagraphs (2) and (3) out of this until we get down to them; let's weed out every *which, said, such,* and *same*; let's cut down on all those varieties of vegetable seeds that are cropping up everywhere; let's make four sentences out of one; and so on. Here is the result:

> On October 30, 1943, Mr. E. J. Murphy (Chief of the Grain Products Branch of the Food Distribution Administration) wrote a memorandum to commercial vegetable-seed growers. He listed varieties of beet, carrot, onion, rutabaga, and turnip seeds and their prices per pound. (These are the prices commercial growers must pay to farmers if they want to sell to the Federal Surplus Commodities Corporation.)
>
> Those prices are now your ceiling prices if you are a farmer-producer. You can add freight charges (by a usual route and method) from your farm to the place where the customer gets the seeds.

And now let's try to "solve" a complicated legal definition:

> Ultimate consumer means a person or group of persons, generally constituting a domestic household, who pur-

chase eggs generally at the individual stores of retailers or purchase and receive deliveries of eggs at the place of abode of the individual or domestic household from producers or retail route sellers and who use such eggs for their consumption as food.

That's a lot of words; let's try to cut down on them. Let's say just "people" instead of "a person or group of persons"; then let's leave out all those clauses with the word "generally" in them (they don't belong in a definition anyway); then let's say "eat" instead of "use for consumption as food." Now let's see what we have:

> Ultimate consumers are people who buy eggs to eat them.

You wouldn't have guessed it, would you?

Chapter XX

THE JUVENILE TOUCH

WHEN people want you to use plain talk, they are apt to ask you to talk so that any schoolboy can understand what you say. Children are the commonly used yardstick for popularization; to most people, easy language and language that's plain enough for a child are the same thing.

Now, what makes a book easy to read for a child? For decades, our schoolteachers have tried to find the answer to this question. They have worked out a dozen and more formulas for grading juvenile books, and have applied these formulas to literally every children's book in print. Supposedly they know all about what makes a book easy for seventh-graders or tough for fifth-graders, and so on.

So far, so good. The only trouble is that the children don't seem to agree with the book-grading grownups. Regardless of formulas, they read what they are not supposed to understand and are baffled by books that should be easy for them. Here is, for instance, a puzzling fact mentioned recently in the *English Journal*: Boys who read and like *Ivanhoe* or *The Call of the Wild* or *Treasure Island* are, on the average, ninth-graders; but *all* formulas agree that these three books are too difficult for any children below eleventh grade—in other words, these famous children's classics are "statistically" on the reading level of sixteen-year-olds.

Now, how is it possible that all these grading formulas are wrong? Clearly, the answer must be the principle they all have in common: they are all built on word counts. Practically all of them are applications of the *Teachers Word Book*, a famous educational tool that has been used by English teachers for over twenty years. In the *Teachers Word Book*. each word has a number; the number shows how often the word is apt to be found in print. The word-count book grader simply checks whether the author uses "common" or "uncommon" words and how many of each. When he is through, he figures out at what grade children are apt to be familiar with most of the words, and the grading is done.

But it so happens that the *Teachers Word Book* was never neant to be used that way. Professor E. L. Thorndike compiled it simply as a guide for teachers to decide how important t is for children to learn a particular new word they find in a book. He did *not* say that the most common words are easiest to understand (*according*, for instance, is common in print but rather difficult); and he did *not* say that words that are infrequent in books are necessarily unfamiliar to children for instance, words like *bowwow, bumblebee,* or *popcorn* are t the bottom of the list).

But the word-count book graders, it seems, never read the preface to the *Teachers Word Book*. To them, any word hat's rare in print is a hard word, and that's that. Doubtless hey would say that to read and understand

Little Miss Muffet
Sat on a tuffet
Eating her curds and whey

equires a Ph.D. degree, since curds and whey are rarely menioned and nobody knows just what a tuffet is.

As yet, they haven't tried to simplify *Mother Goose* by relacing uncommon words by more common ones ("Little Miss Muffet Sat on her chair Eating her milk and cream"). But hey *have* "simplified" a great many other books, among them *Treasure Island*, which, as we have seen, is supposedly far too ifficult for all those children who have enjoyed it ever since tevenson wrote it. Here, for instance, is the beginning f that exciting chapter "What I Heard in the Apple Barrel," adapted for the intermediate grades" with the aid of the *Teachers Word Book*:

"No, I was not the captain," said Silver. "Flint was captain. I was his quartermaster. In that same battle lost my leg, and old Pew lost his eyes. It was a master surgeon that amputated my leg and saved my life. But we hanged him like a dog with the others. It is bad luck to change a ship's name. It always happens that way. I remember Flint's old ship, the *Walrus*. Why, I have seen her loaded with gold and her decks red with blood. The changed her name, and that was her last voyage."

"Ah!" said Dick, the youngest sailor, "old Flint was a great captain. What happened to his men?"

And now let's see how Stevenson wrote it:

> "No, not I," said Silver. "Flint was cap'n; I was quarter master, along of my timber leg. The same broadside lost my leg, old Pew lost his deadlights. It was a maste surgeon, him that ampytated me—out of college and al —Latin by the bucket, and what not; but he was hange like a dog, and sun-dried like the rest at Corso Castle That was Roberts' men, that was, and comed of chang ing names to their ships—*Royal Fortune* and so on Now, what a ship was christened, so let her stay, I says So it was with the Cassandra, as brought us all safe hom from Malabar after England took the Viceroy of the In dies; and so it was with the old *Walrus*, Flint's old ship as I've seen a-muck with the red blood and fit to sin with gold."
>
> "Ah!" cried another voice, that of the youngest han on board, and evidently full of admiration, "he was th flower of the flock, was Flint!"

Let's compare these two versions. What was Stevenso trying to do here? Well, in the first place, he tried to com municate the contents of this passage to the boys for whom he wrote the book. That's a truism, of course, but since th educators tell us that only a fifteen- or sixteen-year-old ca understand *Treasure Island*, let's measure the difficulty o this passage by our own yardstick. It turns out to be VER EASY, fifth-grade reading, understandable to anybody who ca read. That's not surprising, since it's obviously written in simple conversational style, and anyway, most fiction is easy reading according to our scale. So any "adaptation for the intermediate grades" is unnecessary.

But let's go on from here. Stevenson was *not* just trying to tell his readers that Silver was not captain but quartermaster, that he had a wooden leg, and so on and so on. He was trying to tell his story so that important facts would be stressed and stick in the reader's mind; in other words, he was using certain rhetorical devices as they would fit into a sailor's yarn. He writes metaphors like "Latin by the bucket" or "the flower of the flock," and he falls at one point into a clearly rhythmical pattern (" . . . a-muck with the red blood and fit to sink with gold"). As every good writer, Stevenson uses his skill to be not only understandable but effective.

But all that is just the ABC of writing. There is far more to this passage that Stevenson set out to do, and did. A boy is hidden in an apple barrel on a ship and overhears snatches of a conversation between two sailors: what he hears must sound like random pieces of a sailor's yarn, it must have the colloquial touch, and it must smell of the sea. Here is how Stevenson does it: He starts out "No, not I," which implies that a conversation has been going on for some time. Then he skilfully creates the rambling effect by drifting from the wooden leg to the surgeon, from the surgeon to the hanging, from the hanging to Roberts's men, from Roberts's men to changing ships' names, and so on. And then, of course, he makes it sound conversational by putting in "him that ampy-tated me" here and "I says" there, and reminds you of the sea by using sailor's slang like *deadlights* for eyes or *timber leg* for wooden leg. Result: a perfect paragraph that is unmistakably a piece from a sailor's yarn.

And beyond all this, behind all these writing tricks and devices, is the real point of the passage, the thing that is never said but always implied. The chapter before this ends with the words: "It was Silver's voice, and, before I had heard a dozen words, I would not have shown myself for all the world, but lay there trembling and listening in the extreme of fear and curiosity: for from these dozen words I understood that the lives of all the honest men aboard depended upon me alone." And then the chapter "What I Heard in the Apple Barrel" opens with our passage. And the boy in the barrel—and the reader with him—listens, and all of a sudden he knows: "Pirates!" How does he find out? Not just from the words; from something between the words, from sound and atmosphere, from "hanged like a dog" and "Corso Castle" and "Royal Fortune" and "Malabar" and "a-muck with the red blood and fit to sink with gold." Understanding the plain meaning of the words isn't enough; he has to catch on to what this is all about, and he does it by drinking in the sounds of these unfamiliar, exotic, adventurous, half-understood words.

But the people who test the vocabulary range of children's books and rewrite them "for the intermediate grades" will never admit that a boy can understand the meaning of a passage by way of half-understood words. If *Malabar* is not in the *Teachers Word Book,* then it is too difficult for children to understand, and that's that. Out with it. Out with all the words beyond the most frequently printed 5,000, or 2,500, or whatnot. Out with *timber, deadlights, college, Latin, bucket, sun-dried*; out with *Corso Castle, Roberts, Royal Fortune, Cassandra, the Viceroy of the Indies.*

And so, cleansed of all live, colorful, imaginative words we get our version for the intermediate grades. Yes, it's still VERY EASY by our yardstick; but the "flower of the flock" has become just another "great captain"; "a-muck with the red blood and fit to sink with gold" now reads "loaded with gold and her decks red with blood"; there is no rambling sailor's yarn any more, but an orderly, matter-of-fact narrative, neatly tied up with "and that was her last voyage" and "What happened to his men?" Besides, all the transitions have been cut out, so that the whole tale becomes jerky, meaningless nonsense; and the adapters even managed to misunderstand Stevenson's simple prose and write "they changed the *Walrus'* name," when actually "they let her stay what she was christened." It's still easy to read for a boy; but he may have quite some trouble catching on to the idea that Silver was a pirate.

So we see that vocabulary cutting makes a text actually harder to understand. But that is not the worst of it. Actually, if all books were adapted in this fashion, children would never learn any words beyond those they know already: they would never learn the meaning of a word like *broadside* from its context—which is the only natural way of learning new words—because all new words would be carefully eliminated from their reading. In other words, they would forever reread the familiar words of their narrow childhood life and would never grow up in their native language.

Now, of course, children are much too smart to stand for any such scheme. They will go on reading things that are exciting, adventurous, and strange; and they will pass by anything that is prepared and adapted for them by avoiding the unfamiliar and limiting the fancy. To be understood by a schoolboy, you have to use plain talk, to be sure; but you also have to use imagination to dress up what you say, or the schoolboy won't listen.

Suppose, for instance, you have a nine-year-old boy and you want to tell him how to behave while his daddy has gone to war. It may be a good idea to tell him a story about another nine-year-old boy in the same situation; but you will have to work very hard indeed to think up incidents that will keep your boy excited. You will certainly *not* get anywhere if you try to keep him spellbound with this from a recent children's book, *Young Man-of-the-House*:

> "I could be man-of-the-house maybe," murmured Eben, half to himself, "if I could only remember to be."
>
> He must think of something that would help him remember . . .
>
> One day he came home from school to find his mother sorting over Father's clothing, the civilian clothes he had worn before joining the army. Mother was sending some of the suits and sweaters to the cleaner. Others were being brushed and sprayed and hung away in clean muslin bags. At this particular moment Mother was looking over Father's neckties. She placed certain ones in a box

between layers of tissue paper. Others she dropped in a little pile on the floor by her chair . . .

Eben picked up one of the ties that Mother would not keep for Father because she said it was terrible. It was a sickly green, with liver-colored polka dots. Eben couldn't see anything the matter with it. In fact, he thought it was handsome, and as new as if it had never been worn. And indeed it had not, owing to Mother's poor opinion of it . . .

Eben wore the tie to school the next morning, around the neck of his pull-over. "Oh, dear," murmured Mother, gazing after him. "It seems to mean so much to Eben. But what will his teacher think of me, allowing him to go to school looking like that?"

Can you imagine a nine-year-old boy reading eagerly about clean muslin bags and layers of tissue paper? Or about a wife disliking one of her husband's ties? Can you imagine him spending even a minute on a book like this when he could spend it on the funnies, like 93 per cent of all American children? Why should he read about polka-dot ties while Joe Palooka is on a life raft and Terry is on a bombing mission over China? This is what he gets from one newspaper page:

JOE PALOOKA

THEY'LL SEND PLANES OUT T'LOOK FOR US IN A COUPLE OF HOURS.

THAT SURE TAKES A LOAD OFF ME MIND—NOTHIN'T'WORRY ABOUT HUH?

I WOULDN'T THINK SO.

WELL, GUESS I'LL JIST TAKE A LITTLE SNOOZE THEN. I'M KINDA TIRED AFTER THAT BUCKIN' BRONCHO OF A RIDE AN' THEN JUMPIN' TOO.

NO YOU WON'T. WE'RE GONNA SORT OUT AN' LOOK OVER OUR SUPPLIES. THIS SAYS SEA ANCHOR, THIS IS A BAILIN' BUCKET . . . OH BOY—FISHIN' TACKLE . . .

WHAT'SA USE . . . WE'LL ONLY BE OUT HERE A COUPLA HOURS I'M GONNA SLEEP.

GET TO WORK! BREAK OUT THOSE SUPPLIES!!

HEY! YA MUST A BEEN KIDDIN'. WHAT'S EATIN' YA . . . YER WORRYIN' ME NOW . . . D'YA THINK WE'RE . . . WE'RE IN FOR A LONG WAIT?

TERRY

WHEELS DOWN. LOCKED AND SAFETIED. BRAKE AND HYDRAULIC PRESSURES OKAY . . . FLAPS DOWN FULL . . . LANDING LIGHTS ON.

THEY GOT OUR RECOGNITION SIGNALS AND PUT ON THE RUNWAY LIGHTS—BUT WE AIN'T DOWN YET!

WE MADE IT TO THE DRAGON LADY'S INDO-CHINA SPOT. BUT NOW COMES THE TOUGH PART . . .

SECURE YOUR BELTS—STAND BY FOR LANDING!

I'LL TAKE A DESTROYER ON NORTH ATLANTIC WINTER CONVOY *any* TIME!

IF I EVER GET BACK TO KANSAS CITY I'M NEVER EVEN GOIN' UP TO THE SECOND FLOOR OF THE HOUSE!

OH, BOY . . . I'VE BEEN WAITIN' FOR THIS . . . NOW, MAYBE, I'LL GET A SHOT AT A JAP. OH, BOY, OH, BOY!

I am sure the word counters will raise many objections to this. They will say that *hydraulic* and *convoy* are much too difficult for children and should be replaced by easier words. They will point out that the "unfamiliar" word *snooze* is not in the *Teachers Word Book* and should therefore never be used with children. And they will refuse to have anything to do with the comics anyway.

Well, that the comics are VERY EASY—by our yardstick or by any reasonable yardstick you might apply—there can be no doubt. But they are more than that. In the words of the *Journal of Educational Sociology*, "they serve to fulfill the psychological needs of the child . . . Like the folklore of other times, they serve as a means to stimulate the child's fantasy life and so help him solve the individual and sociological problems inherent in his living . . ."

In other words, they supply him with reading matter where the words "Oh, boy!" fit in naturally.

Chapter XXI

ONE LANGUAGE AFTER ANOTHER

PROBABLY the most practical method of simplifying your language is to write and speak as if you were talking to a foreigner—to someone who may be just as smart as you are but who has grown up in another language and hasn't had a chance yet to make himself fully at home in English.

One should think that in the United States of all countries everyone must be familiar with the kind of English that is spoken and understood by the foreign-born. But that isn't so. Most native-born people in this country, in spite of their daily experience with immigrants, firmly believe that a foreign accent and a few foreign words are all there is to broken English. They don't know much about learning foreign languages, and they seem to think that it means just learning a lot of words.

So when an advertising copy writer wants to tell a story in the words of a "little Austrian headwaiter," this is what happens:

> ". . . Paul was a fine boy . . . Paul has a goot home fine clothes, education . . . In high school, he is smart, plays games, dances with the girls.
>
> "Paul goes to University. Nobody says what's waiter's son doin' in University. *Die herren* professors do not ask . . . He gets the diploma *maxima cum laude,* highest honors. My son can walk with learned men.
>
> "We have the war. Paul says he will be a flier. Does the Army say who is this waiter's son who would be *offizier* send him back to the kitchen? No. Paul flies . . . Soon he

is first lieutenant, captain, squadron leader. His letters say he is happy. We do not learn of his honors until later. He dies a hero . . .

". . . If there is peace for good, then Paul does not waste his life. The treaty, the *realpolitik* is only words and papers. Unless we *Amerikaners* make the other peoples believe and hope and trust each other!"

Of course, this is not meant to be a true copy of the way an Austrian immigrant would express himself; but it is obviously what a copy writer might expect people to recognize as a speech by somebody with a German accent. There is a touch of bad pronunciation (*goot*); the present tense is used a little too much; and there are a few German words thrown in. Oddly enough, they are exactly those German words a native American would understand (*Die herren, offizier, realpolitik, Amerikaners*). One of them (*realpolitik*) is a German word that has recently found its way into English, and is used in this ad in a way no German would ever use it. Two other (*herren* and *offizier*) are the equivalents for *mister* and *officer* in German, and would probably be among the first words to be dropped by an immigrant in his daily speech. The fourth word, *Amerikaners,* lends a German touch to what an Austro-American headwaiter would certainly call "Americans," but happens to be not German at all (the German word for *Americans* is *Amerikaner* without an *s*).

Aside from all this, the passage is straight colloquial English. More than that, it is highly idiomatic English in spots, and contains expressions an immigrant would acquire last, like "My son can walk with learned men" or "He dies a hero." The writer, like most other people, simply didn't know that the main feature of broken English is wrong idiom.

Here, for instance, are a few random examples of common errors that are listed in a grammar for German-Americans:

> Oh, I am here already twenty years.
> I didn't see him lately.
> It came all back to me.
> The father said, you must behave.

Are the news good?
I cut me in the finger.
He left without to say good-by.
I must make my hair.
He remembered me to do it.

There is nothing wrong with any of these sentences as far as vocabulary goes. The trouble is exactly the opposite: they are German sentences, translated *word for word* into English. Why do we use *news* with a singular verb? Why do we leave out the article before *father*? Nobody knows. It's the way it is done; it's the way we speak our language; it's idiomatic, and that's that. In German, the word for news is used with the plural and that for father is used with the article, and many German immigrants stick to their German idioms as long as they live.

In other words, to write or speak "correctly broken English" is almost impossible for anybody who isn't born to it. Probably nobody but an Indian could have written this sentence (from Charles Round Low Cloud's "Indian News" column in the Black River Falls *Banner-Journal*): "The weather is change wind every half day and person getting catch cold easy." And nobody but an immigrant could have written this sentence (from George Papashvily's book *Anything Can Happen*): "Rapidly, if one applies oneself, one speaks the English."

But there is one type of broken English that *can* be learned by native Americans, a language with textbooks, grammars, and dictionaries—Pidgin English. As you probably know, Pidgin English is the business language of the Pacific; linguistically, it's English words with Chinese grammar. Since Chinese grammar is extremely simple and has practically no idioms, Pidgin English—or let's say, broken Pidgin English—is easy to pick up. Just to give you an idea, here is the Pidgin English translation of the following English text:

> If you want to kill a pig, you take a dog, a spear, and an axe, and go down to the swamp. Keep going until sunrise. By then you will be very hungry and feel like eating.

In Pidgin English this reads:

> S'pose you like kill 'im pig. Aw right. You catch 'im one-fella dog, one-fella spear, one-fella ackis. Aw right. You go down-below 'long place 'e got water. You go, you go, you go. Aw right, by-'m-by sun 'e come-up on top; belly belong-you 'e hungry too-much. Belly belong-you 'e sing-out 'long kai-kai . . .

As you see, there are a few Chinese idioms, like "one-fella," but the main trick is that every thought is given a whole sentence (like a "s'pose" sentence for an "if" clause) and all idiomatic expressions are replaced by extremely literal explanations; "keep going" becomes "you go you go you go," and "you feel like eating," "your stomach calls for food" ("belly belong-you 'e sing-out 'long kai-kai").

Now, if we stick to the Pidgin English principle—one thought to a sentence, and everything literal rather than idiomatic—we have a pretty good recipe for a sort of universal Imitation Broken English. This is the kind of language a good writer uses for his foreign-born fictional characters. For example, Rose Feld's Czech cook *Sophie Halenczik* talks like this:

> "Kathi is my cousin. She live with me. She and the two children, until her husband get fixed. They come from Europe four months ago . . . They greenhorns. Paul, he is Kathi's husband, he have to hide when the Nazis find out about him. He belong to the Masaryk party . . . We help them. A friend of Paul, he come one day with a letter from Paul and he tell us he can get them out if we have money for the tickets. He don't say where they are; he say it's a secret . . ."

However, if you want to talk so that a foreigner can understand, you don't have to use broken English yourself, of course. As long as you are simple, concrete, personal, and as long as you use short sentences and avoid very idiomatic expressions, you will be all right. Some of the people who teach English to foreigners are pretty good at that sort of thing. The following brief description of the Beveridge plan in the *Weekly News*, the paper for WPA Americanization classes, may give you an idea of what I am talking about:

> FREEDOM FROM WANT IN BRITAIN
>
> Last month, an important report was made to Parliament by Sir William Beveridge. It was the report of a commission to study and make a plan for keeping the people of Britain free from want. The commission has been working for a year. Now all Britain is talking about the report made by Sir William.
>
> The Beveridge plan is a system of social security for everyone in the country. It would give payments for unemployment, old age, and sickness. It would pay the costs of birth and death. All of this would be done by the government for a small tax each week.
>
> The report shows how much the system would cost. It shows, too, how it could be paid for. Some of the newspapers and many of the people of Britain are for the plan. Some believe it is sure to be made into a law.
>
> England is more nearly ready than this country for the widespread social security this plan will give. The war has made great changes there. Four out of five school children get free milk. One in four gets free food. The British have had social security longer and it has given the people more help than social security in the United States.
>
> ---
>
> New words: *Parliament, commission, system, social security, payments, sickness, widespread, birth, death.*

This is not a perfect example of simplification, but it ranks fairly high. In fact, it rates FAIRLY EASY on our scale. It could be improved in spots—for instance by using the active rather than the passive voice in many of the sentences—but on the whole it shows how a complex subject can be explained to foreigners. If you were talking to native-born Americans, however, you could be quite a bit simpler by using idioms wherever possible (Fowler says "Idiom is natural or racy or unaffected English"). For instance, instead of saying: "Some of the newspapers and many of the people of Britain are for the plan. Some believe it is sure to be made into a law," you might say: "Quite a few British papers and a lot of British people are backing the plan. Some feel it's bound to go through."

So, English-for-foreigners is a good model for plain English in general, if you take care to pick the right kind, and add a dash of idiom. But here we come up against a special kind of English-for-foreigners that claims to have a better formula than any other: I mean Basic English. In fact, Basic English has got so much publicity lately that many people think Plain English and Basic English are the same thing. (I wouldn't be surprised if some of you took this book first for another book on Basic.) So let's spend a little time on Basic:

Basic English is a system of simplified English for foreigners that was invented by the British philosopher C. K. Ogden. It has also been proposed as a world language, and as a device for simplifying difficult English. It is limited to 850 words, 200 of which stand for "picturable" things, like "apple" or "knife." There are only 18 "operators" (verbs), namely, *come, get, give, go, keep, let, make, put, seem, take, be, do, have, say, see, send, may,* and *will.* Supposedly, everything can be expressed in Basic, and it's miraculously easy to learn it, both for foreigners and native-born Americans or Englishmen.

From the point of view of this book, everything is wrong with Basic. To simplify your talk, this book first of all recommends short sentences, about which Basic doesn't care. The next item is concrete words, of which Basic has only a skimpy 200, which is a drop in a bucket for anybody's conversational needs. Next, we need references to people, about which Basic again doesn't care. Then we need many, many verbs for plain talk, but Basic hates verbs and has only 18 of them on the menu. And so on, until we come to the special requirements of English for foreigners, which supposedly is Basic's own field. Here we say that the avoiding of idioms is most important; but Basic, with its limited vocabulary and its short list of verbs, has to express practically everything by idioms, and some things even by idioms that are Basic rather than English (*rich* is expressed by the English idiom "well-off," *forgotten* is expressed by the Basic idiom "not kept in memory").

Just for the fun of it, let's see how Basic compares with good, plain English. Among the many books that have been "put into Basic" by and for addicts, let's take a classic model of simplicity: Andersen's Fairy Tales. First, a normal English version of a passage from "The Little Match Girl":

> . . . Lights were shining from every window, and there was a most delicious odour of roast goose in the streets, for it was New Year's Eve—she could not forget that. She found a corner where one house projected a little beyond the next one, and here she crouched, drawing up her feet under her, but she was colder than ever. She did not dare to go home for she had not sold any matches, and had not earned a single penny.

And now the Basic version:

> . . . Bright lights were coming from every window, and there was a very good smell of cooked *goose*,[1] because it was the night before the New Year—yes, that came into her mind. In an angle between two houses, one of which came out farther than the other, she took a rest, seating herself on the sidewalk and making an attempt to keep herself warm. She had put her little feet under her, but she was unable to keep off the cold, and fear kept her from going to her father's house because she had got nothing in exchange for her matches and was unable to take back any money.
>
> [1] A sort of great farm-bird which is made fat for the table.

Now, aside from the illuminating footnote explaining the word *goose* which was not good enough for the select company of 850, there are the following items that make the Basic version ten times as hard to read as the English one: First, there is a great deal of difference between an *angle* and a *corner,* and even more of a difference between a *cooked goose* and a *roasted goose.* Second, the Basic idioms "came into her mind" and "put her feet under her" might be quite baffling to a foreigner. Third, the English idiom "to take back money" is apt to confuse any reader (to take back money you must have had it in the first place). Fourth, and most important, if you want to understand this paragraph you have to deal with abstractions like *attempt, fear,* and *exchange,* and you have to do without such handy, everyday words as *shine, forget, draw, dare, home, sold, earned,* and *penny.* It gives you, like everything in Basic, the feeling of something blurred and out of focus, as if the real meaning were hidden behind a veil.

And in case you doubt that it is actually possible to write difficult Basic English, let me quote this one sentence by C. K. Ogden himself:

> A third step on the same scale would be a Basic Parallel Library of 1,000 books giving the Basic form of the works of great writers of the present and past and on the opposite page the words of the writer himself, so that everyone would at least have a chance of learning any language in which he might be interested, with the help of Basic Notes on hard points to make the use of one of the Basic Dictionaries, which are now being got ready for all the chief languages, very much less frequent than at present.

According to our yardstick formula, this sentence is VERY DIFFICULT. And this is where we leave the subject of Basic English.

Chapter XXII

THE FUTURE OF PLAIN TALK

AFTER twenty-one chapters about plain talk, you can easily guess what this last one is going to be about. I called it "The Future of Plain Talk," but that's just a title. It's really the what-does-it-all-add-up-to chapter no book of this kind can be without.

Let me first say a few words about the yardstick formula you find in this book. Maybe it seems an odd device to you; probably you never heard of a similar approach to writing. But that's only because up to now this type of research has been buried in educational journals and dissertations and you had no chance to get acquainted with some of the tools of modern psychology. There are a number of "readability formulas" that have been worked out, and doubtless there are more to come. The one here is, I think, easy to apply and useful for most practical purposes. After a while, you will get the feel of it and you will be able to guess difficulty levels pretty accurately, using the formula only as a check. In any case, you will probably fall into the habit of focusing on the language in which things are said, and often you will find yourself quite naturally "translating down the scale" as you go along.

The main use of the formula, as I see it, is as a laborsaving device. More often than not nowadays, writing is done on assignment, and usually the most important part of the assignment is to make information readable for the people it is meant for. However, there has never been an adequate way of checking a writer's performance on that score. Theoretically, it would of course be possible to interview a sample of prospective readers to see whether they understand the stuff or not. This sort of thing has occasionally been done; advertising firms have learned to avoid the word *dentifrice* in their questionnaires, and public opinion pollsters have found that the phrase *free enterprise* is apt to be misunderstood by three out of ten Americans. But since it is impossible to pretest in this fashion everything that is being written, the specifications for simple-language assignments are usually "Put this in one-syllable words" or "Leave out all five-dollar words" or some other meaningless generality. When it comes to material that is not clearly slanted toward the lowbrow, it is ordinarily assumed that correct grammar and usage are all that is needed. Hardly ever do people realize that simple, easily readable language means time and effort saved at the receiving end—that is, by all those professional and specialized people who have to do a tremendous amount of reading every day. An hour spent in simplifying the style of some memorandum or technical paper may save thousands of those busy people five minutes of their time. Figure this out in dollars and cents and you will see what I mean by laborsaving device.

But, of course, writing is still far from being as professional and efficient as all that. There are now, according to the census, 70,000 people in this country who make their living by writing—more than there are shoemakers or fishermen. They have outdistanced these two trades in number, but they are still way behind them in technical skill. Specific writing jobs are still being performed by the methods of our forebears; in fact, beginning writers are being taught to take pride in following long-accepted style models. Composition, as it is being taught in our schools and colleges, is something that has to do with Edmund Burke and Charles Lamb and so on—in other words, with literature. I don't mean that a liberal education is not a good thing to have; but to write an operation sheet or a house organ, you have to know how, and it generally doesn't even occur to grownup people that the literary kind of writing they have learned in school might be of help. When they are faced with a practical writing job, they just go ahead and make a mess of it, or else they try to get advice from those writing schools and magazines and handbooks that promise quick training to the amateur. But this is not the answer either. Usually the emphasis there is entirely on the how-to-earn-an-extra-thousand-dollars aspect of writing, and it is taught as a game rather than as a profession and a science. The results are often funny. One advertisement for a famous handbook on writing says: "Writers, speakers, business men, and everyone who wants to use the English language as it should be used, *needs* this helpful guide." Another ad for a well-known writers' magazine starts with this: "There Is No Magic Wand!—*which* we or anyone else can wave to make you a writer in ten easy lessons." The point I want to make is not that *need* and *that* (or no pronoun) in these two sentences would be "better grammar"; the point is that these ads by so-called experts are not as readable and effective as they could be.

Back of all this is our whole attitude toward language and understanding. Most of us still seem to have the primitive notion that understanding language means understanding words, and that understanding words means "to know what they mean." If you have a good-sized vocabulary—that is, a store of words, plus their meanings, neatly filed away in your brain—then you will be able to understand almost anything, and the world will be your oyster. Or, in the words of the *Reader's Digest*, "each new word you learn will increase your mental power. There may be other ways to success, but vocabulary building is the easiest and the quickest one." Unfortunately, this just isn't so, and the cash value of words like *minions* and *panegyric* is practically zero. Language is not as simple as all that and we understand words not by way of "vocabulary building" but by way of their contexts. If this were not so, simple writing—or any writing, for that matter—would be very easy: you just cut out the big words, and there you are. As we have seen, this actually *is* the method of the word-count addicts, and the Basic English people, and, in fact, most writers of simplified stuff—and it never works. To simplify contexts and not just words is another matter, and I hope that after reading this book you will have some idea of how it is done. (I hope you will also have some idea of the beauty of simple prose, but this is beside the point.)

Scientific language simplification could be used in many

other ways than just for making writing more efficient. For instance, plain talk (I mean generally understandable standard-level English) could be adopted as an interscientific language, so to speak. What I mean is this: As everybody knows, each science nowadays has its special language, and it is practically impossible for members of one branch of science to understand what members of other branches are talking about. This is no great trouble in the physical sciences, where technical terms are usually clearly defined; but it is a tremendous problem in the social sciences and the humanities, where each word seems weighted down with connotations that are familiar to those in the know but impossible for an outsider to guess. Even two closely related sciences like sociology and psychology are as far apart in their languages as this:

From the *American Sociological Review*:

> By heuristic schematisms and devices, we may be able to establish functionally a concept of the social individual which may meet the requirements in investigating the dynamic variations within the ideal-typical patterns to which we should ordinarily address ourselves.

From the *Journal of Social Psychology*:

> In the case of an account which squares with fact, not only will the writer of it experience meaning, but the reader of it can effect an intra-organismic closure which will, or could, be testable for him.

Now, since it would be an obvious advantage for sociologists to know what psychologists are doing, and vice versa, it might be worth while to bridge the gap by translating certain scientific papers into standard American.

Usually, this kind of suggestion is being made by people who want to make fun of scientific language or "debunk" it. I don't mean it this way. I don't see why scientists shouldn't use specialized language as a sort of shorthand among themselves. But, on the other hand, I think that translation within a language may be just as important as translation from one language into another.

It is true, of course, that after simplification it often turns out that "the Emperor has no clothes on." That's a common thing to happen, and there are plenty of such examples in this book. The reason is, I think, that it is easier for most people to juggle vague and empty words than to be concrete and specific in what they say. This "Gresham's Law of Language" seems practically irresistible to half-educated people and school children. As one English teacher says, "adolescents in high school manifest an almost incurable tendency to indulge in highfaluting abstractions. Since their learning has been chiefly of a verbal nature, they proudly parade the fruits of their schooling by displaying at every turn their mastery of hallowed stereotypes." I think training in simplification methods might be a good antidote for that.

Recently, a movement has been making headway that tries to go much further; those who believe in semantics are fighting against the "tyranny of words" in general and have denounced *all* abstractions as meaningless fictions. Here is a typical paragraph from a book on semantics:

> The man on the street who says there "ain't no justice" speaks more truly than he knows. There has never been any such thing. Justice is a Fiction, along with its fellows —Friendship, Discipline, Democracy, Liberty, Socialism, Isolationism, and Appeasement. You cannot point to their referents . . .

Now that, it seems to me, doesn't get anybody anywhere. To say that all these big words are abstractions is simply a truism; anybody can look up *justice* in the dictionary and find that it was formed by adding *-t* to the Latin word *jus* (right) to make it an adjective and then adding *-ice* to make it a noun. In other words, most parts of that word don't "mean" anything but are just empty grammatical gadgetry. However, since our language happens to be built that way, we cannot just go ahead and banish all those words from our speech (which seems to be the dream of the semanticists). Also, we would have to draw an arbitrary line somewhere and say, This is a fiction and this is not, and to do that we would have to accept the language-is-a-heap-of-words fallacy I talked about before. Otherwise, there is no reason why we should stop at weeding out the big abstractions everybody recognizes as such anyway; why not also throw out *but, like,* and *though,* or those chief troublemakers among the little words, *and/or, if any,* and *unless*? In other words, what semantics adds up to is simply that our ordinary language is a poor instrument of thought and communication, and that we shouldn't take its devices too seriously.

I thoroughly agree with the semanticists on this point. In fact, I cannot imagine anybody doing any rewriting and simplifying without realizing that language is, at best, a crude and arbitrary system of symbols and that we cannot understand anything as long as we mistake words for things. This kind of error is the source of most prejudices and irrational arguments. Let me quote just one example (from the article on "Theology" in the Encyclopædia Britannica):

> The great doctors from Tertullian to Aquinas who have expounded Trinitarian doctrine were feeling for a mode of being intermediate between what can be denoted by a noun and what can be denoted by an adjective, such as an attribute or a relation. Since human experience knows of no such mode of being and the conception of it cannot be elucidated by any analogy, these teachers have recognized that, in the last resort, they were dealing with mystery or with what transcends the limits of the human mind to comprehend or to conceive.

What do you think a Chinese would think of this passage, or anyone else whose native language does not differentiate between nouns and adjectives? Surely, he would diagnose it as pure nonsense, as a typical example of mistaking words—or in this case the syntax of Western languages—for the things themselves. This passage deals with medieval scholasticism, whose modern followers, the neo-scholasticists, are the chief mistakers-of-words-for-things these days. But they are not the only ones by any means. There seems to be a vast number of people who have to be told that, as Robert Louis Stevenson put it, "the world was made before the English language and seemingly upon a different design."

This common lack of understanding for alien languages and ways of thinking brings us to the problem of an international language. I am one of those people who think that English has already won the race and that sooner or later it will be officially adopted as *the* world language. But that doesn't settle the question of what *kind* of English is going to be used. If English can be spoken or written on many different levels of abstraction or difficulty, then naturally the adoption of just "English" wouldn't do and a specific level, say FAIRLY EASY, should be chosen for use in international meetings and documents.

I know that this is just a dream. Nobody will ever stop diplomats from using the complex idiom known as diplomatic language. But even so, the linguistic approach to international documents might help. It would at least make us realize the level of abstraction of certain international agreements—in other words, the degree to which they are agreements at all. Maybe a linguistic analysis of the Atlantic Charter would have made it less of a shock to the world when it turned out that the Charter was an agreement on words rather than deeds or, as Churchill said in his speech on India, that it "does not try to explain how the broad principles proclaimed by it are to be applied to each and every case which will have to be dealt with when the war ends . . ."

The use of FAIRLY EASY English for international affairs would mean nothing else but the use of conversational, everyday language for settling arguments; as everybody knows, only the thrashing out of things around a conference table is apt to produce agreements that really work. In other words, colloquial, easily understandable language is the outward sign of the use of democratic, peaceful methods of settling disputes. This holds true in domestic as well as in international affairs; in fact, democracy could be defined as government by plain talk. Or, in the words of John Dewey, "the heart and the strength of the democratic way of living . . . are the processes of effective give-and-take communication, of conference, of consultation, of exchange and pooling of experiences—of free conversation if you will."

APPENDIX

HOW TO USE THE YARDSTICK FORMULA

1. *Pick your samples*

Unless you want to test a whole piece of writing, take samples. Take enough samples to make a fair test. Don't pick "good" or "typical" samples. Go by a strictly numerical scheme. For instance, take every third paragraph or every other page. Each sample should start at the beginning of a paragraph.

2. *Count the number of words*

Take each sample and count each word in it up to 100. Count contractions and hyphenated words as one word. Count as words numbers or letters separated by space.

3. *Figure the average sentence length*

Find the sentence in each sample that ends nearest to the 100-word mark—that might be at the 94th word or the 109th word. Count the sentences up to that point and divide the number of words in those sentences by the number of sentences. Do this for each sample. In counting sentences, follow the units of thought rather than the punctuation: sometimes sentences are marked off by colons or semicolons instead of periods—like these. But don't break up sentences that are joined by conjunctions like *and* or *but.*

4. *Count the affixes*

An affix is "an addition placed at the beginning or end of a root, stem, or word, to modify its meaning" (*Oxford Dictionary*). However, if two words are combined into a compound word (like *baseball*) neither of the parts is considered an affix.

Count all affixes in your samples up to the 100-word mark. (If your text has more or less than a hundred words, compute the number of affixes per 100 words.) Affixes may be inflectional endings, prefixes, suffixes, or foreign endings. The most common affixes are listed on pages 197 to 201. However, these lists are not exclusive. They do not contain rare affixes, like -aign in *campaign.* On the other hand, do not count mechanically everything that looks like an affix but is part of the root, like -er in *matter.* If you are in doubt, check the word derivation with a dictionary. (The *Concise Oxford Dictionary* is handiest for this purpose.)

Count affixes in proper names (for instance, the -ite- and the -d in *United States*) except where the original meaning has been completely lost (don't count the -er in *Fannie Farmer* or the -ine in *Argentine*).

Exceptions: Do not count -es or -s when used to form plurals, possessives or the third person singular. Do not count -en when used to form plurals. Do not count ending -d or -t in *could, did, had, might, ought, should, stood, went, would.*

5. *Count the personal references*

Count all personal references in your samples up to the 100-word mark. If your text has more or less than a hundred words, compute the number of personal references per hundred words. Count the following three types of personal references: names, personal pronouns, and the words listed below that deal with human beings or relationships.

Names: Count all names of people or animals (first names, last names, nicknames, petnames, etc.) Count the full name with titles as one personal reference.

Personal pronouns: I, me, my, mine, myself; (thou, thee, thy, thine, thyself); you, your, yours, yourself, yourselves; he, him, his, himself; she, her, hers, herself (count also if referring to a ship or country); we, us, our, ours, ourselves; they, them, their, theirs, themselves (count only if referring to people).

Words that deal with human beings or their relationships: Man, woman, boy, girl, child, baby; father, mother, son, daughter, brother, sister, uncle, aunt, nephew, niece, cousin; husband, wife, sweetheart; family, parent, dad, daddy, papa, mamma; mister, mistress, miss, gentleman, lady, sir, madam(e), lad, lass, guy, dame, kid; people (not peoples), folks; friend, fellow, pal.

This list is exclusive. Do not count any other words, like *teacher* or *doctor.* But count combinations of the listed words with each other and with grand-, great-, step- and -in-law. Count also familiar forms of these words, like *grandpa.* Count singulars and plurals.

·. *Average your data*

a. Add the average sentence lengths that you found in your samples nd divide the total by the number of samples used. This will give ou the average sentence length for the whole piece of writing.

b. Add the number of affixes in all your samples and divide the otal by the number of samples used. This gives you the average umber of affixes per 100 words.

c. Add the number of personal references in all your samples nd divide the total by the number of samples used. This gives you he average number of personal references per 100 words.

'. *Figure your score*

Use the yardstick formula:

Multiply the average sentence length by .1338 ....

Multiply the average number of affixes per 100 words by .0645 ....

Add

Multiply the average number of personal references per 100 words by .0659 ....

Subtract

Subtract the constant .75 ....

Your score is ....

(The multiplications are worked out for you on pages 202 to 204.)

Check your score against the QUICK REFERENCE TABLE n p. 205.

.IST OF COMMON AFFIXES (PREFIXES), WITH EXAMPLES

- about, amoral, avert, achieve
b- abhor
bs- abstract
c- accord
d- admit
f- afford
fter- afternoon
g- aggressive
l- allocate, already
ambi- ambiguous
amphi- amphibian
an- anarchist
ana- anatomy
ant- antagonize
ante- antedate
anti- antitoxin
ap- appeal
apo- apostasy

ar- arrive
arch- archbishop
archi- architect
as- assign
at- attain
auto- automobile
be- beguile, because
bene- benefactor
bi- bicycle
bio- biography
by- bystander
cata- catalog
cath- catholic
circum- circumference
cis- cisatlantic
co- cooperate
col- collateral
com- commemorate
con- connection
contra- contradict
cor- correlation
counter- counteract
de- deduce
di- dilemma
dia- diagnose
dif- different
dis- dismiss
dys- dysentery
e- eliminate
ec- eccentric
ef- effect
em- embargo, emperor
en- enchant
enter- entertain
eph- ephemeral
epi- epigram
equi- equidistant
es- escort
eu- eulogy
ex- exaggerate
extra- extraordinary
for- forget
fore- forecast
hemi- hemisphere
hetero- heterogeneous
homo- homonym
hyper- hyperbole
hypo- hypotenuse
i- ignorant
il- illiterate
in- inactive, into
infra- infrared
inter- intersection
intra- intramural
intro- introduce
ir- irritable
mal- maltreat
mega- megaphone
meta- metamorphosis
mis- mistake
mono- monograph
multi- multiform
neo- neolithic
non- nonchalant
ob- obstacle
oc- occur
of- office, offer
off- offset
omni- omnipotent
on- onslaught
op- oppose
ortho- orthodox
out- outline, outlive
over- overcome
pan- panacea
panto- pantomime
para- paraphrase
pen- penultimate
per- percolate
peri- periphery
poly- polysyllable
por- portrait
post- postscript
pre- precede

pro- proceed
pseudo- pseudonym
pur- purpose
re- revise
red- redeem
retro- retrospect
se- secession
semi- semicircle
sub- subsoil
subter- subterfuge
suc- succeed
suf- suffer, suffice
sug- suggest
sum- summons
sup- suppose
super- superhuman
sur- surrender
sus- suspender
syl- syllogism
sym- symbol
syn- syntax
tele- telephone
thorough- thoroughfare
tra- tradition
tran- transcendental
trans- transatlantic
tres- trespass
tri- triangle
ultra- ultraviolet
un- unlock, until
under- understand
uni- university
up- upset
vice- vicepresident
with- withdraw, without

LIST OF COMMON AFFIXES (SUFFIXES AND FOREIGN ENDINGS), WITH EXAMPLES

(Combinations of two affixes are marked "2")

-a area, idea, opera, data
-able suitable
-aceous (2) rosaceous
-acious (2) vivacious
-acy (2) fallacy
-ade lemonade
-ae alumnae
-age marriage
-ain certain, captain
-al cereal, real
-an American
-ana Lincolniana
-ance abundance
-ancy (2) pregnancy
-ant hesitant
-ar liar
-ard drunkard
-arian (2) librarian
-arium (2) aquarium
-art braggart
-ary commentary
-ate activate
-ation operation
-cide homicide
-cle cubicle
-cracy (2) democracy
-crat aristocrat
-cy bankruptcy
-d said
-dom freedom
-ed lived
-ee employee
-eer pioneer
-eign foreign, sovereign
-el hotel, shovel
-en fasten, golden, written (not: happen)
-ence inference

-ency (2) tendency
-ent competent
-er teacher, folder, better
-ern northern
-ery pottery
-es series, mores
-esce coalesce
-escent (2) adolescent
-ese Chinese
-esque Romanesque
-ess princess
-est highest
-et pocket, violet
-ete obsolete
-etic energetic
-ette cigarette
-ey alley, money
-ferous (2) vociferous
-fic specific
-fication (2) amplification
fold manifold
-form uniform
-ful beautiful
-fy testify
-gram monogram
-graph phonograph
-graphy (2) photography
-hood childhood
-i stimuli
-ial facial
-ian Bostonian
-ible edible
-ic basic
-ical (2) logical
-ice service
-ics antics
-id stupid
-ide bromide
-ie movie
-ier soldier, financier
-ies species
-il civil
-ile fragile
-im victim, interim
-in insulin
-ine gasoline
-ing walking
-ion division
-ique technique
-is crisis
-ise treatise, merchandise
-ish finish, English
-isk asterisk
-ism Fascism
-ist egoist
-it limit, unit
-ite polite, unite
-ition nutrition
-itis arthritis
-ity authority
-ium premium
-ive creative
-ize criticize
-kin manikin
-le twinkle, battle (not: little)
-less endless
-let booklet
-like childlike
-ling duckling
-logy (2) criminology
-ly cleanly, daily, slightly, onl
-m poem, phlegm
-ma stigma, coma
-me scheme, theme
-meal piecemeal
-men specimen
-ment achievement
-meter diameter[1]
-mony (2) alimony
-most topmost
-n been
-nd errand, reverend
-nda agenda, propaganda

-ness greatness
-nomy (2) economy
-o ratio
-ock hillock
-od method, period
-oid celluloid
-ol phenol
-on criterion
-one ozone
-oon balloon, cartoon
-or doctor, sailor
-ory factory
-orium (2) auditorium
-os chaos
-ose verbose
-osis (2) apotheosis
-ous famous
-phile Anglophile
-ry dentistry
-scope microscope
-ship dictatorship
-some handsome
-son reason, prison
-sophy (2) philosophy[1]
-st first
-ster gangster
-stress seamstress
-th wealth, faith, fourth
-t draft, height, meant
-tion portion
-tude multitude
-ty ninety
-ue value, issue
-um forum
-ure nature, future
-us nucleus
-ute minute, statute
-verse universe
-vert extrovert
-ward(s) afterward(s)
-ways always
-wise likewise
-worthy (2) praiseworthy
-x apex, vertex
-y[2] very, breezy, army, beauty, city, dolly

[1] In words like "diameter" and "philosophy," which seem to be made up wholly of affixes, choose one affix as the root, and don't count it.

[2] Count -y also when it appears as -i-; for example—"ladies," "business," "hurried." Do not count -y in "any," "body," "every," "many."

SENTENCE LENGTH

Multiplication table for use with the formula

Average sentence length in words times .1338

1	.13	31	4.15
2	.27	32	4.28
3	.40	33	4.42
4	.54	34	4.55
5	.67	35	4.68
6	.80	36	4.82
7	.94	37	4.95
8	1.07	38	5.08
9	1.20	39	5.22
10	1.34	40	5.35
11	1.47	41	5.49
12	1.61	42	5.62
13	1.74	43	5.75
14	1.87	44	5.89
15	2.01	45	6.02
16	2.14	46	6.15
17	2.27	47	6.29
18	2.41	48	6.42
19	2.54	49	6.56
20	2.68	50	6.69
21	2.81	51	6.82
22	2.94	52	6.96
23	3.08	53	7.09
24	3.21	54	7.23
25	3.34	55	7.36
26	3.48	56	7.49
27	3.61	57	7.63
28	3.75	58	7.76
29	3.88	59	7.89
30	4.01	60	8.03

AFFIXES

Multiplication table for use with the formula

Number of affixes per 100 words times .0645

1	.06	31	2.00	61	3.93
2	.13	32	2.06	62	4.00
3	.19	33	2.13	63	4.06
4	.26	34	2.19	64	4.13
5	.32	35	2.26	65	4.19
6	.39	36	2.32	66	4.26
7	.45	37	2.39	67	4.32
8	.52	38	2.45	68	4.39
9	.58	39	2.52	69	4.45
10	.64	40	2.58	70	4.51
11	.71	41	2.64	71	4.58
12	.77	42	2.71	72	4.64
13	.84	43	2.77	73	4.71
14	.90	44	2.84	74	4.77
15	.97	45	2.90	75	4.84
16	1.03	46	2.97	76	4.90
17	1.10	47	3.03	77	4.97
18	1.16	48	3.10	78	5.03
19	1.23	49	3.16	79	5.10
20	1.29	50	3.22	80	5.16
21	1.35	51	3.29	81	5.22
22	1.42	52	3.35	82	5.29
23	1.48	53	3.42	83	5.35
24	1.55	54	3.48	84	5.42
25	1.61	55	3.55	85	5.48
26	1.68	56	3.61	86	5.55
27	1.74	57	3.68	87	5.61
28	1.81	58	3.74	88	5.68
29	1.87	59	3.81	89	5.74
30	1.93	60	3.87	90	5.80

PERSONAL REFERENCES

Multiplication table for use with the formula

Number of personal reference per 100 words times .0659

1	.07
2	.13
3	.20
4	.26
5	.33
6	.40
7	.46
8	.53
9	.59
10	.66
11	.72
12	.79
13	.86
14	.92
15	.99
16	1.05
17	1.12
18	1.19
19	1.25
20	1.32
21	1.38
22	1.45
23	1.52
24	1.59
25	1.65
26	1.71
27	1.78
28	1.85
29	1.91
30	1.98

QUICK REFERENCE CHART

Description of style	Difficulty score	Words in average sentence	Affixes per 100 words	Personal references per 100 words	Typical magazine	Potential audience (Typical audience one step below)	
						School grades completed	Percent of U. S. adults
VERY EASY	up to 1	8 or less	22 or less	19 or more	Comics	4th grade	90%
EASY	1 to 2	11	26	14	Pulp-fiction	5th grade	86%
FAIRLY EASY	2 to 3	14	31	10	Slick-fiction	6th grade	80%
STANDARD	3 to 4	17	37	6	Digests	7th or 8th grade	75%
FAIRLY DIFFICULT	4 to 5	21	42	4	Quality	Some high school	40%
DIFFICULT	5 to 6	25	46	3	Academic	High school or some college	24%
VERY DIFFICULT	6 and up	29 or more	54 or more	2 or less	Scientific	College	4½%

Index